To Delores,
thank you for
Your [illegible]
[illegible]

DADDY TALKS:

Empowering Fathers, Encouraging Children and Equipping Families

BY

TONY E. SANDERS, JR.

#theABundantLife

Published by Best Seller Publishing®, Pasadena, CA

Best Seller Publishing® is a registered trademark

Printed in the United States of America.

ISBN 978-1-946978-21-9

This publication is designed to provide accurate and authoritative information with regard to the subject matter covered. It is sold with the understanding that the publisher is not engaged in rendering legal, accounting, or other professional advice. If legal advice or other expert assistance is required, the services of a competent professional should be sought. The opinions expressed by the authors in this book are not endorsed by Best Seller Publishing® and are the sole responsibility of the author rendering the opinion.

Most Best Seller Publishing® titles are available at special quantity discounts for bulk purchases for sales promotions, premiums, fundraising, and educational use. Special versions or book excerpts can also be created to fit specific needs.

For more information, please write:

Best Seller Publishing®

1346 Walnut Street, #205

Pasadena, CA 91106

or call 1(626) 765 9750

Toll Free: 1(844) 850-3500

Visit us online at: www.BestSellerPublishing.org

Acknowledgments

I want to first thank God for the gift of life and the privilege to be a part of something that is bigger and greater than myself. Because of the gift of life and the giftedness that I have been blessed to possess, I am able to be a gift to others. This book is just one expression of my gratitude and one example of me giving to others, what has been freely and generously given to me.

I would like to thank my wife of 23 years, Shawntrice Sanders, for her support and encouragement. Not only did you give me the freedom to discover and pursue my life purpose, you stuck by my side in the process. A great deal of gratitude goes to my children, who are the reason that this writing exist. Had I not had the privilege to be their daddy, I would not have much to say or much to share. Thank you for filling the void and allowing me an opportunity to break the cycle and break the silence.

To my mother (Valda Beck) and grandfather (Willie J Branigan), may they both rest in peace, I dedicate this book in their honor. They were two people that believed in me and showed great pride in my accomplishments. To my grandmother, Amanda Branigan, this book is also in your honor, as you have always been my biggest cheerleader and supporter. Without you, none of this would be. Your encouragement and love has been more valuable than any riches, fame or fortune. Thank you, for being you.

To my church family I owe a great deal of gratitude. You have allowed me to be me and have accepted me, as is. You allowed me to grow up and grow into the leader that I am today and you never judged or abandoned me as I learned while on the job. There have been special members and friends that have been trying to push this work out of me, for quite some time. You know who you are. Thanks for staying on me and staying on my side. There is much more to come. Stay tuned.

Last but not least, I dedicate this writing to my father (Anthony E Sanders, Sr.). He was not the father that I wanted and expected him to be, but he is my father. I am happy to share, that after this book was sent to the publisher and days away from print, I was able to reconcile with my father and many of my concerns shared in this book have been addressed. I look forward to providing my readers with an update, with this book's sequel *(Daddy Talks: Let the Healing Begin.)*

Table of Content

Introduction

Daddy Talks is a book that in part, shares talks that a father had with his children, while at the same time it is an example of a father who attempted to break the stereotype of silence that is often attached to fatherhood. *Daddy Talks* is a collection of talks shared between a father and his offspring, but even more so it is a chronicle that shares and shows the power of a daddy who talks. For when he talks, what he has to say, is something that can positively shape and mold the lives of his seed. Likewise, his silence can begin an avalanche of brokenness and bitterness that not only affects the lives of his children, but his lineage and the state of the family. This author contends that if more daddies will open up and talk, the trajectory of families and community will forever be changed.

Motive and Motivation, behind the talks

Over the past 22 years, I have served as a pastor and life coach. Throughout that time I have had countless sessions with individuals that have either shared their great frustration with their father, often described as "a man of few words" and with those that confessed that their father just failed to share pertinent life tips or failed to engage in conversations that would prepare them for life or help them to succeed in life. As I listened to numerous males and females open up about their "fatherless" experience, I realized that I too shared their experience. I recalled numerous occasions where I found myself ill-equipped or uninformed on certain matters and how ashamed I felt that I had not been taught things that young men should have been taught or should know. I quickly came face to face with my past and in that encounter I discovered a great deal of hurt and humiliation. There was the pain of not having a father and not having that paternal nurturing and instruction. The pain of not having a live-in male figure that protected the house, provided for our household and who was present to guide and guard our family. While many of my peers experienced the same void, there were quite a few that did have fathers or at least had malefactors that taught them and talked to them. And this both confused me and infuriated me. They had an advantage that I didn't have and an experience that I could not relate to. A present and engaged father was foreign to me and as a result, I felt a sense of emptiness and ignorance. Though there was nothing that I could personally do to change that, I could change my future and work to break the cycle. I decided that I could do one of three things: I could use the state in which I found myself as a justifiable excuse to succumb to a life of underachievement; I could continue the same irresponsible behavior by demonstrating the same actions toward my children or I could determine to break the cycle by breaking the silence and flipping the script. My 20 plus years of parenting and this book are the fruit of the latter.

This book contains a collection of talks that I wish my father would've had with me and in turn, I had with my children. And by me sharing it in written form, I am affording others an opportunity to glean from my decision to break the cycle. This writing does not boast to be an exhaustive guide on all that there is to share nor suggest that these are the only things that a father should share. Rather, it is merely the things that this father felt was most important and urgent for his children.

These talks were my search to have something to say that might be of help, as we prepared our children for independent living and a family of their own. It also was an attempt to find my way to effective parenting. Since I didn't have that father figure in my life, I felt inept to be a father. Therefore I didn't know what true fathering looked like or what I was supposed to do. I thought about the things that I had to learn, as a man, and thought about the things that I wished were shared with me. By default, these thoughts became my parenting guide. I now knew what to say, based on what was not said to me. I thought about all of the embarrassing moments that I had, both as an adolescent and as an adult, where I knew nothing about certain topics or lacked certain "manly skill sets." These were the times where I would often say, "I wish I had a father to groom and guide me." These were the occasions where I realized that something was missing and if I didn't come up with something, it would continue to be missing and my children would be just as lost as I was, even though their father was present. While it was good that I was at least present in their lives, I asked myself, what is different and/or what difference is my presence, if I do not impart some form of wisdom and direction. For me, *Daddy Talks* was an answer to those questions and helped me to find resolve. Please note, some daddies are present, but do not talk. And when daddies are present and do not talk, it is just as hurtful and harmful as fathers that are absent or choose to abdicate their responsibility or abandon their children. In some cases, it is far more damaging and hurtful. Our children need to hear the father's voice. Our society needs Daddies to talk.

I am certain that others could add more topics and teaching points and may even suggest that the ones that I focused on are less important than other points. That may be so and I do not debate or argue against it. I just know that there was quite a bit that I was not told and I in turn wanted to make certain to tell my children, something. *Daddy Talks* is that something. I hope that you enjoy it and find that it is helpful. If you are a father and struggles with having talks with your children, feel free to use these topics as a jumpstart. If you are a child, whether grown or still growing, and you never had a father that "talked," feel free to extract whatever you can from this father/child dialogue and make a determination to be an "intentional parent" and begin to parent on purpose. Happy reading.

Meet the author

My name is Tony E Sanders, Jr. I was born in Sulfolk, England. My grandfather was in the United States Air force and while stationed overseas, my mother visited he and my grandmother. While there, she went into labor and my journey officially began. I was classified as a dual-citizen, since I was born in Great Britain, but on a US military base. Some 17 years later, when I decided to serve in the military, it was necessary for me to declare my citizenship. Since I was six months of age, I lost my British accent and didn't have any British friends, I chose the great U S of A ☺

At the time of this writing, I can officially declare that I have been married to my wife for over two decades. I have 5 children, 4 of which are all well into their twenties and one who is a senior in highschool. I currently pastor a church, am an entrepreneur, owning multiple small businesses and I am a community activist. I have served my community in numerous capacities and currently am the president of the city's only ecumenical and interdenominational ministerial alliance. I provide life coaching and consulting and offer services to courts and jails and assist offenders through restorative justice efforts.

I have traveled abroad, as a guest lecturer, workshop facilitator, keynote speaker, consultant and participant in archeological excavations. As an author, I hope to use my platform and product to enhance my services and to empower others.

CHAPTER 1

Who Are You?

Who am I? Do any of us really know? Well, I guess that depends on who you ask and how you determine what defines or makes up one's true identity. I am sad to admit, but while growing up, I had no idea who I was. And not knowing who you are, hampers and hinders what you do and what/who you become. Realizing this, I had to dig deep and search wide, to discover me and to define me. In doing so, I realized that this was another area where I longed for male input and could benefit from a "daddy talk." Nonetheless, I had to figure it out for myself. Unfortunately, many are not as fortunate in figuring this out for themselves and most of their lives, if not all, is wasted in a cycle of confusion and a series of choices that result in mental, emotional and even physical distress.

In my attempt to prevent my children from having an identity crisis and in my intent to break the cycle, I included this topic into my daddy talks. My own personal self-discovery was not easy, nor was it quickly attained. I struggled, suffered and sought for significance, inclusion and relevance. This was a lonely quest and a painful one. During this search, I learned a great deal about my fears and my insecurities. I discovered that I was afraid of being alone, though I was comfortable with being a loner. I feared rejection and dismissal. I feared it so much, that it was to the extent that I sabotaged many relationships. Though it was done unconsciously and unintentionally, it was an attempt to protect my heart and feelings. I felt that if I let people too close to me and allowed them to stay too long, that they may get to know the "real me" and wouldn't like me or would leave me. Or worse, that they would hurt me.

Though I was a family man, I had determined that I would never marry. I feared others knowing me and that fear kept me at a healthy distance, as I held others at bay. This journey took me on a rollercoaster of a ride and forced me to deal with things that I didn't realize had anything to do with my identity. I had to deal with the things that hurt me, the things that haunted me, as well as the things that helped me and "hoped" me. All of these things and experiences contributed to how I was shaped and in their own right, made me who I am. So many are accustomed to deducing their identity to their name, gender, culture and maybe even their geographical locale or socio-economic status. When in actuality, all of the aforementioned are important and contribute to one's identity, but fall shy of fully defining one's self.

In addition to what was discussed in the previous chapter, spirituality, one's identity is inclusive of understanding and embracing their nationality, sexuality, physicality, individuality, mentality and personality. All of these things, help to make us who we are and therefore tells us and others, who we are. Once again, I do not claim to have penned an exhaustive list nor do I deem myself as having all of the answers. I have merely shared what I deemed to be most relevant and pertinent to the discussions had with my children and that I considered as a starting point for discovering self.

Daddy Talks... (daddy talks are the actual words imparted to my children)

- **Nationality**

  Part of our identity and knowing who we are, is knowing from whence we've come. Humanity's national origin has become so diluted, that it's nearly impossible for anyone to know with absolute certainty their most pure ancestry. But for the most part, we have some indicators that we use and based upon those, we side with or claim a specific heritage. For all practical purposes, we hail from Ham, one of Noah's sons and are of African descent. Our most recent ancestry is from North America, more particular, the United States. Because of this dual origin, I am most comfortable with our family being identified as African American. This may not be what is most popular and many debate on what the most appropriate classification or nationality is. Once again, for me and for our household, African American seems most appropriate.

  It is important that you understand and connect with your heritage. For in it, you discover who YOU are. Though our heritage and culture has been pretty much diluted, as a result of the trans-Atlantic slave trade and American slavery, it is important for us to grasp hold of remnants that help to define and describe us. It is helpful in better understanding yourself, better understanding your behaviors, better understanding your mannerisms, better understanding your expressions, better understanding your ideology, better understanding your context, better understanding your contribution globally and much more. You better appreciate where you are and where you are going, when you better understand where you come from. The wealth of information and knowledge attained is invaluable and it helps to make sense out of life.

Once you better understand your nationality, you unlock the door to self-pride, and appreciating your value and self-worth. You are able to take note of who you are, because you notice whose you are. Take notice of who you are and take great pride in whose you are. Never allow anyone to define you or determine your worth. You were created in greatness, you were made from greatness, you come from genealogical greatness and you are destined for greatness. So gain knowledge and be great!

- **Sexuality/Sensuality/Gender Identification**

   Sexuality is a very important component in understanding who we are and in understanding ones identity. It heavily influences the way you live and the role that you play in the life that you live. It will influence not only your life, but will influence the life of your family and determine how your household is reared. You will nurture your children, based upon how you are "natured" and large in part, how you were nurtured. Your true nature speaks volumes to who is presented to the world and impacts what contribution you make in this world. It is important to exude modesty and self- respect, when expressing or presenting yourself. The saying, "if you got it, flaunt it" does not reflect good judgment in character or taste and you shouldn't want your appearance or actions to misrepresent you. That being the case; cover it, contain it and control it.

   How you see or define yourself, heavily influences how you treat yourself and how you treat and interact with others. Gender classification is not as clear cut and straight forward, as it once was. Gender identity is very important as it molds your beliefs and behaviors. And it influences what you teach to your children. Get a clear understanding of who you are, as it relates to your gender, and learn to control your sexual and sensual urges.

As human beings, we have the ability to discern and discriminate in what we do and who we do it with. We are not wild and untamed animals and have common sense. We have the mental capacity to make responsible and sound decisions. Though your emotions may run rampant and your urges may be strong, you have the ability to control yourself. You must maintain integrity and discretion, in all that you do and you must protect your body, preserve your body and present your body in a manner that is appropriate and that promotes a positive brand. Not only are you your brand, but you are a walking billboard and a living resumé. When people see you, they size you up and make determinations and assessments about you. Therefore, always be in control of your image, as you write your script.

• **Physicality**

Whether it is fair or not fair, people will make determinations, form opinions and judge you, based upon your physicality. Some aspects of your physical appearance, you have no control over, while others areas are totally in your control.

For example, you cannot control your height, natural skin tone or physical features, unless of course you go the route of medical alterations. So for all practical purposes, you are stuck with what you got. And since it was divinely given to you, accept and appreciate it. "You are fearfully and wonderfully made" and without mistake. You were created on purpose and with a purpose and your physical make up was part of that intentional design. Never allow trends, fashion or societal pressure to cause you to be unappreciative or question how you were naturally made and or look. You are unique and beautiful and NEVER forget that or let anyone tell you different.

There are some things that are somewhat cosmetic or superficial and perhaps you may desire to enhance or alter, but never let it *be because you think there is something wrong with you or that you are inferior. If for health reasons or for personal fulfillment you need to add a few pounds or shed a few, there is nothing wrong with that. How YOU choose to wear your hair or accent your features is your choice. And know that at the end of the day, no one is perfect, but we all are perfectly made by design. Meaning, your build, texture, tone and dimensions are what they were intended to be by the intentional hands of the Creator Never doubt yourself or second guess your worth or identity, because it may be different from the status quo. Be yourself and be happy and content with who you are and what you look like. Beneath the exterior is where the greatest gems are housed. Your personality, character, intellect, compassion, disposition and giftedness should outshine and/or add value to your physical appearance and they should complement one another.*

Though you cannot control your natural physical features, you can and should be very mindful of your exterior and how you physically present yourself. What you wear, how you wear it and what you look like, as it relates to your appearance says a lot about you and sells you. Not only are you your own brand, you have only one chance to make a first impression. Therefore, always try to make your first impression a lasting, positive and memorable one. Never cheapen yourself or lessen your value, by embracing the "if you got it, flaunt it" mentality. Always choose modesty and moderation.

There are many liberties that you may have, but that does not mean that you should take advantage of all of them. Many things might be legal and within your liberty, but not all things are prudent or gives you a free license to act and live irresponsibly. Modesty, morals and moderation should be the filters used when making decisions. Take pride in who, what and how you represent yourself.

Daddy talks end here...

In this postmodern world where many will suggest that there are no absolutes, rules seem to be archaic and "the norm" is loosely defined, our youth have a strong proclivity to be drawn toward an unguarded and unhealthy sense of independence. To the extent that many buck and shun against authority and accountability. Parents and in particular, fathers, must reclaim and reestablish some sense of order, to instruct and direct our youth. Lest we lose our youth. What better way, than for more daddies to begin talking and in those talks, coach our sons and daughters to reach their full potential and live productive lives.

CHAPTER 2

Character vs. Characters

*True character consist of integrity, honesty, responsibility
and dignity. To lack any of these virtues, compromises
one's character. Be committed to be well-rounded and be
committed to being a person of character.*

• • •

S omeone has rightfully suggested that the definition of character is, "who you are, when no one is watching." What many fail to take into consideration, is that it is easy and convenient to be on your best behavior, when others are paying attention, but what really matters is what is done when no one is paying attention. To only act appropriate when there is an audience, is to be disingenuous and instead of being a person of character, one is merely *living as a character*. Unfortunately, we live in a world filled with charlatans and chameleons.

While folk are going to ultimately do whatever they want to do, you cannot dismiss the value in having someone to direct you and instruct you. Those initial directives and set of instructions are to come from your parents. While my mother did a very good job at advising me on how to conduct myself, it was void the paternal influence. The contribution that my mother made to the child rearing experience was obviously of great substance, as I am who I am today because of how I was raised and because of who raised me. However, there were certain things that my mother was just not equipped to do and that was to help me to develop into a man. I know that there is a trend that has been going around for many years, whereby mothers are heralded as mommy and daddy and are even wished a Happy Father's Day on this annual day of acknowledgment. While to some, it may sound cute and seem appropriate, it's one of the most disregarding, disrespectful and delusional gestures made and in my opinion, fuels the increasing dysfunction, dissolution and dismantling of masculinity. But that's another book in and of itself.

It is rather sad that so many fathers have left their families and in doing so; they have left their families to fend for themselves and for the mothers to double-up in responsibility and parenting. Countless mothers have held it down and have done a phenomenal job in making the best out of a bad situation. Nonetheless, they are not fathers. Yes, they have had to be an all-inclusive parent, but anthropologically and anatomically speaking, they are not "fathers." And because they are not, they cannot raise a man. They can however, raise a gentleman and groom a respectful and respectable human being, who can in turn innately become who he was created to become. But only men can make men and model manhood, therefore it is imperative that "daddies talk."

But there is also a very important role that fathers play in the lives of their daughters. While of course, fathers cannot teach their daughters to be women, for all of the same reasons that I used against mothers raising men, fathers do play a very significant role. Fathers affirm and provide a great deal of validation. They also mold their daughters and model what healthy relationship and interaction should look like, between opposite genders. Fathers set the tone and fashion the template. From this, daughters either gravitate toward or run away from men that remind them of their father-daughter interaction. It is crucial for fathers to take this role seriously, as many young ladies grow up to be women that seek and search for their daddy, in the men that they choose. The father sets the standard and wherever he places the bar, will heavily influence what their daughters will expect or accept. As fathers, we must set the bar high and make certain that the standards are appropriate as well.

Here I found myself, once again, in that awkward position of wishing I had the masculine perspective to direct me and to sit me down and advise me, like I witnessed on *The Cosbys*. How I longed that the man to man bonding moments and instructional moments between Cliff and Theo were actual captured moments of me and my father. Interesting enough, the lessons shared on this sitcom were being absorbed by me, on the other end of the television tube and I was vicariously being raised by an actor and activist who was merely pretending and playing a role on a TV show. Though I couldn't personally relate to the Cliff/Theo relationship, I liked what I learned and how it made me feel and longed for the same type of relationship. To the point, that I now had a template in which I could use to incorporate into my parenting. In addition to his relationship with his son, I was able to glean from the relationship with his daughters and even his wife. This provided me with a context that influenced and modeled my role as dad, husband and as a man.

What I learned from Cliff, my virtual dad and male figure, was healthy interaction between father and son, father and daughter and husband and wife. And how ironic, that I learned character, from a person playing a character. Amongst many other things, I learned how to be a person of character and in turn was able to teach this virtue to my children and model it in my household.

Part of being a man, is to put away childish things and to think and act like a man. In other words, Man-UP! I began to do that and it resulted in me learning and demonstrating; responsibility, honesty, integrity and dignity.

Responsibility

I have always had a very playful and joking side to me. I love to laugh and I love to make others laugh. Playing practical jokes, telling jokes, being silly was something that I truly enjoyed and as a result, people loved being around me and desired for me to be a part of their festivities. The party didn't get started, until I arrived.

As I got older, however, and as I had taken on more responsibility, I found that my "funny bone" wasn't what it used to be. The demands and expectations that had been placed and even forced upon me had begun to bring about a different person and it wasn't a person full of smiles and jokes anymore. The role of father, now a minister, family man, emerging community leader and somewhat of a dominate figure in my immediate family who was expected to "hold things down" had somewhat silenced my funny side and brought out a more serious and somber side.

I was still funny and had a joking side, but it didn't emerge as often as before. What also seemed to disappear was my patience and my tolerance level began to diminish. I didn't put up with as much as I did before and I was too easily irritated. To some I was considered to be a grump, somewhat mean and no fun anymore. I guess we all respond to responsibility differently.

For me, all eyes were on me and I had a point to prove. And that point was, I was not my father and would not become my father. You see, my father was a big kid and for the most part, never became an adult. Not a responsible one at least. He never owned up to not stepping in and stepping up, in my life. And he never demonstrated responsibility, before me. And I was so adamant about not being a replica of him and repeating his irresponsible ways that I shifted into beast mode. I somewhat lost my charming nature and my personality changed. Simply because I wanted to be a responsible man and a respected father.

As I now look back upon it, I guess I was somewhat bitter. Bitter because of all the pressure that my mother put on me, the expectations that the community placed on me, the demands to be "holy" and the fear of failure. I now had a family of my own that I had to care for. And I was now confronted with juggling between trying to be a man while not becoming a certain type of man. I didn't know how to become that man that I knew I needed to be and I didn't know how to not become the man that society and science said I was most likely to become. What a dilemma. While trying to win, by being different than what I was exposed to, I was losing because I didn't have the template of what to work toward.

I now was wrestling with my emotions and trying desperately to make sense out of life and the new roles that I played. I was upset that my father wasn't present, while at the same time happy that he was absent. Upset, because I didn't know what I was doing and I blamed him for not being there to show me. Happy that he was absent, because he didn't have the capacity to show me anything different than what he had displayed in his own life. So in some regards, it was good that he wasn't around. It was likely that I would have gravitated toward and taken on his irresponsible ways, as this is what I would have been introduced to, "taught" and saw modeled before me. In actuality, he did me a favor by being ghost.

I did find a solution to this problem though. I decided that since he was not able to teach me how to be a good father, a good husband, a good family man and a well- respected community figure, that I would simply flip and rewrite the script. I decided that I could be the man that I dreamt and desired to be, by being opposite of what I had seen. Between my biological father and my step-father, which I haven't even addressed, I witnessed domestic violence, drug abuse, drug use, drug sales, street life, pimps, prostitutes, promiscuity and prison life. My family life was far from the Huxtibles, I tell ya. Since I clearly knew that this was not the family that I wanted to raise, the type of man that I wanted to be and this was not the life that I wanted to live, I made a pact with myself and God, at an early age. I would not try to justify waywardness by pulling the "fatherless child" card. Rather, I would be and do totally opposite of what I had experienced and been exposed to. I would not hit a woman and would vow to never be in a relationship where domestic violence was tolerated. I would not have kids that I did not personally raise and take care of. I would not live a life where I was in and out of jail and absent from my family. I would not be caught up in the drug world and would not be criminal. In other words, I would be totally opposite of my "fathers" and would be a responsible man, by taking care of my responsibilities.

Perhaps this chronicle may come across as me being rather mean, critical and unfair, when referring to my father. And I am certain that many will take that position. But please know, I am not attempting to bad mouth or bash him, I am just telling the truth. And as I attempt to influence the positive exchange within the realm of fatherhood, I can't do so by sugar coating and skirting around reality. And reality is, my father dropped the ball when parenting me. It is what it is. No shade intended. I have to be honest with myself and about my experience, as I try to be healed and healthy so that I can be helpful.

Truth be told, these thoughts and reflections are appearing on the page because they are surfacing as I am writing. Until now, this very moment where I am typing, my transparency is also my therapy. This is not something that I penned and later massaged. These are raw thoughts and feelings and have never been uttered before, until now. I am healing as I am helping others. You are seeing and hearing this at the same time that I am. I never cared enough to really form or articulate these thoughts before. To be honest, I didn't even plan on going in this direction. But in talking about responsibility, I guess I hit upon something and struck a nerve.

Overall, my father is not a bad person. I've heard numerous stories about him from others. And truthfully, many of those stories were positive and often made mention of how kind, soft-spoken and cool he is. That's nice to hear and I am happy that there were those that had good experiences with him. However, that didn't change the fact that he took the absentee route and abdicated his responsibility to others and abandoned me in the process.

In summary, I'm not the best dad, but I would like to believe that I am a better dad to my children, than my dad ever was to me. In part, because I chose and accepted responsibility. I chose to be present and I am choosing to talk. I guess what I am trying to say is, Above all, BE RESPONSIBLE! BE PRESENT! And BE INVOLVED! Daddies, talk.

Daddy Talks...

> My children, it is important to always handle your business. Part of being an adult is being responsible and it is imperative that you learn to do so, now. Being responsible means that you learn to manage your life and take care of your affairs. Never put anything in your name that you do not keep close watch over. Your name is your badge in life and serves as an access card. Protect it and wear it proudly. You ought to be proud of your name and proud when your name is called and mentioned in public. That was not always the case for me. I used to be so embarrassed of my name and cringed when it was called in public. Why, because I bear the same name as my father. And because of his criminal background and the name he had made for himself in the streets, I didn't want anything to do with it and didn't want anyone to know my name. And since I couldn't change my name, I had to find a way to change the name that was made. I became very touchy when my name was mentioned and began to seek out ways to change that feeling I got.
>
> I always dreamt of having a son of my own and wanted to give him my name, but I had a problem. I didn't like my name. I

wanted a son that would proudly bear the name of his father, but how do I do that, if I didn't proudly bear the name myself? So I decided that I would work very hard to bring honor to that name and one day pass it on to my seed. I desired and decided that since I couldn't change my name, I would "change" my name. So instead of the name being associated with crime and irresponsibility, it would carry with it respect, honor, integrity and dignity. Insomuch, that my son would be proud when the name was called and not ashamed, as I was. Son, I hope and pray that this is the case.

I want you, my daughters, to swell up with pride because of your last name and because of who your daddy is. This became my quest and I've been working hard, to make it a reality. I am hopeful that what I have demonstrated thus far, has shown you what it means to be responsible. I pray that you've seen enough that you can use it as a template to guide you. I by no means have been the epitome of what responsibility looks like and what it means, but I have made attempts and given you an idea.

Bottom line is, if you make a promise, keep it. If you get a bill, pay it. If you take a stand, stand your ground and if you make a commitment, see it through. Be responsible.

What others think of you is very important, but what you think of yourself is paramount. You must have a healthy sense of confidence and self-worth, but must be careful to not be arrogant or filled with pride. Do not be guilty of thinking more of yourself, than you ought. Be a person of character and do not settle for being a character. To front and pretend to be something that you are not or more than what you are, is not genuine. Be happy with yourself and within yourself and do not allow the opinion or expectation of others to cause you to compromise or cower. Be a person that you are comfortable living with and able to look at in the mirror. Choose character, over being a character.

- **Respect**

Some argue that respect is something that you earn, while others contend that it is something that should be demanded. Some ascribe that in order to get it, you must give it. I am not going to advocate or argue either position, as perhaps there is some truth in both of them. What I will simply say is, if you do not respect yourself, how can you expect or demand that others do? Respect is something that originates within. If you have internal respect, it will show externally and at bare minimum people will be able to sense where you stand. If a person can see and sense that there are certain things that you do not tolerate or stand for, they have information to act upon and are able to discern how to approach and treat you. Now what they do with it is something totally different, but at least they know.

My children live a respectful life. Have the highest and upmost respect for yourself and by all means, demonstrate respect toward others. Once you have established standards and guidelines for yourself, you will have armed yourself with a guide on how to live and you will have set the stage on how you treat others and how you expect to be treated. You ensure, that when interacting with others, that they put some "respekk on your name." (Misspell intentional. The youth understand the reference)

Once you set your standards, never lower your standards. You do not compromise who you are, for no reason and for no one. While you may need to make compromises as you negotiate through life, never compromise who you are as a person. If you have to settle on or for something, let it be because it was for the greater good. Not because it is all you are worth. Once you have established a set of morals and values, don't be swayed and don't be played.

Some people will try to sway you away from your moral center and challenge your value system. They will try to convince you that it is ok to deviate and veer a little. Don't believe the hype. Your moral compass should never be manipulated or recalibrated to accommodate convenience or selfish desires. Once they are set, stick to them. Nor should you allow anyone to play you, because of your moral center. People will try to use your conscious against you and take advantage of you, because they will interpret your meekness as a weakness. Don't be played.

Being respectful also means to be honorable and to show honor towards others. As an honorable person, be a person of integrity and always maintain your dignity and ensure that you do not take away another person's dignity. Always do what you do because it is the right thing to do. When you do, not only will your intentions remain pure, but you will minimize the disappointment that will come when people do not reciprocate the same back towards you. When you do things for the right reasons, you don't expect anything in return and you are able to do things on your own terms and turf. But when things are done to be seen or because you expect that others will extend the same courtesies toward you, you set yourself up for disappointment. More often than not, you do not get the same in return. Bottom line; do unto others as you would have them to do unto you.

- **Be Honorable**

Be honorable and be honest. When a person has attained a certain level of high public esteem, fame or glory, they are well respected and honored by others. Insomuch that they are extended favor and are considered distinguished. In some instances, it comes along with the position that one holds, but more so it is something that is bestowed upon a person because of their own personal merit, integrity and accomplishment.

We most often, out of respect for the office, refer to our judges, mayors, governors and presidents as honorable and will use this handle when addressing or introducing them. It is because of the reverence and regard that we hold for the position that they hold.

Whether you ever hold such an office or not, you should strive to be honorable, honest and receive honor from your colleagues, constituents, community and your co-horts. By being a person of integrity, you stand a part and are set a part from the average. When others deviate, bend, take shortcuts and cut corners, your commitment to doing the right thing, even when no one is watching and when you can get away with doing the opposite, will speak volumes to your character and will contribute toward your classification as most honorable.

Be mindful that your gifts and giftedness can and will create great opportunities for you. And because of them, certain doors will be open to and for you. Let it not be so, that your gifts take you where your character is unable to keep you. It's one thing to get "there" but another to stay there. Your character, integrity and honor will help you maintain good standing and can present you before and make you most honorable amongst great men and women.

- **Be Dignified**

Likewise, always maintain dignity. Never allow the drive and desire for accomplishment to cause you to be undignified or to loose dignity. Some people will do just about anything to "arrive" or to be accepted and approved. Refuse to let that be your narrative. There is nothing wrong, per se, with wanting to be accepted and to receive the approval of others, unless it comes at the cost of your dignity. Once you have discovered and determined your self-worth, never sell out and never allow a price tag to be placed on your character. Your character should never be for sale and never compromised or negotiated. This should and must be a lifestyle for you and not something that is done out of convenience. When you are a person of high character, you do not have to audition to become a lead character. The natural you, will get the attention, accolades and accomplishment that you seek. At the end of the day, choose character and maintain dignity, at all cost.

CHAPTER 3

Dollars and Sense

Spend time learning about the power of money, instead of just spending money. And don't just make dollars, make sense. When you begin to understand the dynamics of dollars and how to properly use them, you can begin to travel down a path where you are not merely rich, but wealthy.

• • •

P art of being a person of character and being a person with character, is to protect your character (name.) For a good name is far more valuable than great riches. Your name is far more important than providing people with a handle to refer to you by, rather it says who you are. To be clear, not the name itself, but the name that you have made for yourself. Your name reveals your credibility and reliability, in the eyes of the greater society. When you are seeking employment, the employer looks up your name. When seeking to establish credit, the lending agencies look up your name. When determining where you want to live, your name determines what options you have, when determining where you can live. The name that you have made for yourself, precedes you and will influence and dictate your quality of life. If you decide to open and operate your own business or firm, your potential customers and clients will base their decision to do business with you, upon your name and/or the name associated with your business or brand. The reviews, the ratings and the relationships you have established in the marketplace will help you to flourish or fail. So at the end of the day, make a good name for yourself and protect it. This will greatly impact your dollars and it makes good sense.

Whether we realize it or not, our credit score says a great deal about us and can either open doors or close them. Anymore, you can't even attain employment or housing, without a decent credit rating. Why, because it says to others who you are and how you handle yourself and your affairs. And it helps them to determine how much trust or responsibility that they should extend toward you. How you handle your finances and bills, gives insight about your character, your priorities, your reliability and your responsibility. It also dictates and determines what options or opportunities will be made available to you. Your name/financial standing will determine what type of car you buy, where you buy that car and how much you ultimately will pay for that car. So it is, with your housing and other key purchases. Some people have to settle for far less or end up paying much more, all because they didn't realize how important a good name was and instead of being frugal, they were frivolous and foolish when it came to their fiduciary responsibilities.

Daddies must tell their children about the importance of protecting their name, in particular protecting their credit score and being good stewards of their resources.

Daddy Talks...

> *My great grandmother use to always say to me, "save some for a rainy day." I didn't fully understand nor appreciate it then, but I sure do now and wish I had taken heed to her words of financial wisdom, sooner. My mother used to also say to me, "you just can't wait to spend your money. It's like fire and burning a hole in your pocket." Again, words of wisdom that I wish I had listened to and learned from. Too often, people find themselves*

with very little to nothing to show for the work that they've done and/or time, effort and energy that they have exhausted. They will work long and tedious hours at a job, but often are without any fruit from their spoil and sweat equity spent. Either because they have wasted, mismanaged or quickly spent their harvest. How you treat your seed, will determine what the outcome of your harvest will be. To ensure that you have a great harvest, you must learn and incorporate good stewardship and sound money management principles. While I do not claim to have the business acumen of a Bill Gates or Warren Buffet, there are some things that are common sense and just basic knowledge, when it comes to household and business management. I encourage you to research and read upon the ins and outs of financial planning, sound investments and business practices. But for now, I give these simple and elementary nuggets.

- **Save**

The animal and insect instinct for food storage is not only an important biological adaptation, but a good model of survival. During periods or seasons of drought and or depravation, one's existence is contingent upon their survival skills. We can learn a great deal, from many animals, when it comes to such survival skills. From the fowl of the air, to the field mice and frogs, food storage is key. They, like many other animals, by instinct gather food to reserve and ration out appropriately. This not only ensures their existence, but the existence of their offspring. In like manner, many insects do the same thing. From spiders, to crabs, crayfish, termites, bees and beetles, resources are attained and stored up during the winter and bad weather months.

If the insects and animals have sense enough to store up their resources, to ensure their existence and to prevent extinction, then it goes without saying that sophisticated human beings ought to do the same thing, with their resources. My children, you have access to many resources. The earth is a limitless resource that will and can produce whatever you need. Once you know how to work it, it will yield a great harvest that will supply your every need.

When it comes to commerce, you have to know how to leverage it so that you are not merely working for it, but learn to make it work for you. Part of that wisdom is in saving and storing some for later. Depending on what career path you choose, your health and the condition of the nation, you are allocated only so many years that you most likely will devote toward work. While able to work, it is imperative that you use wisdom when handling your wages. It ought not to be imbalanced, as to where everyone else receives and benefits from the fruit of your labor. If you are working to just pay bills and hand your hard earnings over to someone else, then you are truly missing out and will have a hard time surviving the latter years of life.

The government will automatically take what they have established to be their fair share, right off the top. After which, you should sow back into the eternal work manifested here on earth, through the financial support of your local church. And then, you should pay yourself. Your bills and other expenses are then taken care of, out of the remains. If you do not pay yourself, upfront, then you will be at the back end and may end up getting the short end of the stick…from your own earnings. Value yourself enough, to take care of yourself. There ought to be an appropriate amount allotted for you to enjoy now and later.

You should not have to worry about how you will be provided for, when you are seasoned and in the golden years of life. After having spent your youthful days exerting strength and energy and giving society your most vibrant years, the last thing that you should have to be concerned about is making ends meet.

After retirement, you should be able to do what you want to do, not what you have to do. It doesn't make much sense, if your dollars and cents are not available when you need them most. Save some time and save your life, by saving some of your resources for your latter days.

• Budget

Just as important as saving a portion of your resources is, so is budgeting your resources. Budgeting is essential to good stewardship, as it speaks to your level of responsibility and helps to ensure sustainability. If you are not able to sustain yourself, you won't be able to survive. When you have a higher conscious and a deeper level of understanding, you think differently and therefore you live differently. Your choices are influenced by this heightened level of thinking and everything that you do is done in respect to the universe and your role in it. With that being said, you understand that the money that you earn may belong to you, but is not yours. It is to be saved, shared and sown.

Reserve what is needed to survive, but be generous enough to ensure that the less fortunate are cared for and that the money seed is planted in good work and God's work. With this type of thinking, it is important to make certain that your stewardship is sound. You have rights to the money, but you don't have a right to be careless with it. It is your choice to do so, but elevated consciousness protects you from being foolish and prohibits you from squandering your resources. In the process of budgeting and balancing your books, you should be able to see exactly where your money is going. You must determine and dictate where it goes. If you do not, it will go everywhere but where it is used best. And the only part of it that you will see, is it going past you and into the pockets of others. Someone once poetically said, "Money does talk, I can't deny. I heard it once, it said bye-bye." Someone else once said, "A fool and his money are quickly parted." Don't be a fool and don't sit looking and listening to your money, pass you by. It all starts will budgeting and learning to properly manage your money. And when you have proven yourself to be responsible, you will discover that one of two things, if not both will happen. Either you will have extra resources available, because you have freed your dollars up. Or, you will be extended greater opportunities, because you have demonstrated financial responsibility. People that have great resources are people that have learned to keep their money. They are frugal and demonstrate fiduciary responsibility. They of course have also learned the power in having multiple streams of income, sound investments and good business practices. The most basic of them all, is budgeting.

Learning how to budget and living on a budget, is a sign of responsibility and maturity. It also shows how much restraint and discipline one has. As mentioned in the daddy talk about sensuality and sexuality, we are not animals that have no restraint. Our lives ought not to be guided by emotions, urges and impulse. We have the ability to practice delayed gratification and learning to budget and living on a budget is an example of that. We must budget with a purpose and budget on purpose. It's a choice and a choice that you must make, if you want to be successful.

- **Invest**

  Merriam-Webster *submits this definition for the word, invest; "To put (money) to use, by purchase or expenditure, in something offering potential profitable returns, as interest, income, or appreciation in value." Similarly, it also states, "to use, give, or devote (time, talent etc.), as for a purpose or to achieve something." My children, find good soil to invest in and in doing so, you will see a great return on your investment. Learn the difference between investments and expenses. If there is no profitable return, it's not an investment. If you merely expended resources and the return yields no profit, you just merely paid for something and exchanged money for service or goods. It's not an investment. The exchange of services for what you pay, is an expense and should be treated as such. And there is nothing necessarily wrong with that. There are things that we want and need and they cost. But to confuse expenses with investment is costly and foolish. The end result is that you will be a consumer, who makes others profit, while you become poorer.*

The great Midwestern oracle, Warren Buffet, said that "the greatest investment is in oneself." Don't fail to not invest in yourself. Start investing in yourself by exposing yourself to teachings and trainings in an array of topics and subjects. Get education, attend seminars, enroll in mastermind groups, watch webinars and attend conferences and workshops that add value and that teach principles and perspective. In addition, learn to invest in areas that can bring a return that will benefit you and your personal interest. Whether it is in the stock market, your own business venture or someone else's business, make your money work for you and make your money produce a return. Invest, invest and invest some more.

- **Pay bills on time**

While this might sound trivial and thought to be common sense, many have proven this simple principle to be not as commonly practiced or exercised. The importance and power in paying bills on time is two-fold, at minimum. Not only does it protect your name/credit, but it ensures that you are not throwing money away because of late fees and interest. Many people fail to realize that there is a great cost, for not being prompt with their payments. Over a period of time, those fees add up and those are dollars that could be used for something that you want or need. It doesn't make sense, to pay more than you have to. Especially, when it can be avoided. So pay on time and avoid costly consequences of late payments.

Credit cards can be useful and convenient, but they can also be problematic when you are not responsible and fail to practice the principles that have been shared in our daddy talks. Yes, there are some services and goods that are only extended to you, if you have plastic. And in today's technological age, more and more things are moving to online or some form of smart pay. So I of course see and understand the role for credit cards. However, there are a few basic things that you should know, before you go...and spend. Your name/credit score will determine what cards you qualify for, what your annual percentage rate will be and how much credit will be extended to you. In determining this, they will look at your financial history. They want to know who you have done business with, how did you handle your business, did you pay on time, what your spending habits are, do you have more going out than you do coming in, what is your debt to income ratio, amongst other things. So as you can see, it is not just as simple as applying for a card and going on a shopping or spending spree. There are some things that you must take care of, before receiving that plastic and there are some things that you must do, once you do receive it. One of those things is, to pay your bills on time.

Attached to your card, as is the case on any line of credit that you receive, is a monthly interest fee that is accessed. And if you are not careful and wise, the interest can become rather costly. If you carry a balance and fail to pay in a reasonable time frame, you may find yourself getting into a snowball of debt. I suggest, as any responsible financial advisor would, that you pay your balance off as quickly as possible. Preferably within 30 days. That way you are not carrying a balance, your card/ credit line is freed up and you are not getting sucked into paying interest. There are credit repair and credit building tips and tricks that many might suggest, like paying after 31 or 32 days etc. Whatever the case, pay on time and beware of the fees and small print.

While using debit and banking cards are a good option and alternative, there are some things to beware of when using them as well. There are those that use their cards excessively and carelessly and I classify them as:

1. *Idiotic swipers (spending more than you should);*
2. *Irresponsible swipers (spending more than you have);*
3. *Illogic swipers (spending more than it's worth);*
4. *Impulsive swipers (spending more than you realize).*

Idiotic swipers *spend over their budget and use their credit line to purchase things that are not in the budget or that they cannot afford.*

Irresponsible swipers *spend more than what they actually have, because they rely on credit protection and a line of credit that will allows them to go over their limit.*

Illogic swipers *spend more than it's worth because they do not wait on sales, do not shop around for best prices and they use the convenience of the card to make purchases that do not make sense. Regardless of the cost, because of their credit line and their failure to not practice delayed gratification, they have a tendency to make immediate purchases, even if the cost is higher. They also will pay more than it's worth, because their credit line allows them to and or if they do not have the actual funds, they* *rely on their credit protection and therefore pay more than it is worth in fees.*

Impulsive swipers *spend more than they realize, because they just swipe and do not pay attention to how often they swipe and fail to reconcile their account.*

My children, beware of the swipe syndrome. If you are not careful and conscious, you will get used to swiping and will swipe all of your resources away. The convenience of swiping works against us, if you are not disciplined and if you have not developed good practices. It is too easy to swipe your card and the ease and convenience of it can lead to some very destructive behaviors. So be careful and beware. A few things that I have found to be helpful, that I have incorporated into my financial stewardship and that make sense to me are:

- **Choose to pay cash**

  Many people do not like to carry cash anymore. For some, it's a safety issue while for others they prefer the convenience of cards or checks or even PayPal. And that's fine and makes sense, for those that prefer. But I do encourage you to pay flat out and pay up front. There may be many that would suggest other options and some may even be more sound than what I am passing on to you. But if you have the ability to just pay flat out cash, do so. Though it doesn't have to be literally in cash. Cashier's checks and other options accomplish the same thing and I encourage you to consider such options. My rationale behind this goes far beyond the traps of credit cards and lines of credit. It has more to do with exercising good budgeting practices and practicing delayed gratification. If you do not have the hard cash to acquire whatever it is that you wish to acquire, I suggest that you wait until you do. Again, it is way too easy and convenient to pull out that plastic card and get it now. But to demonstrate restraint and say no I will come back when I have the tangible money, shows discipline and the ability to practice delayed gratification.

As already stated, paying in cash does not mean that you literally have to walk around with large sums of cash. Cashier checks are a good option or this is where prepaid cards come in handy. You have the ability to load the exact amount of your purchase on the card and once you spend it, it is spent. As opposed to your debit card, though it may come directly out of your account in real time. When using your debit card, you have direct access to the rest of your resources and sometimes the temptation to spend is too great. And everyone is not mature enough to fight the temptation of a sale or urge. By having a card that has additional resources, you very well might find yourself in a tug-of-war at the register.

Additional reasons why in some instances, I prefer the preloaded card option; is because I am able to choose how much is on there, I have the option to reload when I need it and when I am forced to use a card for auto-pay, I don't have to worry about the creditor taking more than they should. I have personally had some very bad experiences when giving creditors direct access to my primary account. Not only have they made mistakes that have been costly and embarrassing to me, I have found myself at a loss. Sometimes they will refute correcting their wrongs or refuse to pay fees accessed, if other debits have been impacted. So my resolve has been to use this option and protect myself and my resources.

You of course can choose to use all that I have suggested or choose some other options. I am merely providing you with nuggets that will hopefully give you a sense of direction. And giving you far more than what I had. My father didn't tell me anything about any of these matters, so I had to find out the hard way. You do not have to deal with the same obstacles that I did, as I have paved a path that makes your journey a little easier and less stressful. Having the right information and knowing how to use it, not only eliminates unnecessary struggle, but propels and projects you further ahead. At your age, I didn't have the knowledge or the mentor. And as a result I was forced to play catch up. You have been given both and therefore have leverage. You have a head start advantage that if used properly, can take you to far greater heights than I was able to reach.

- **Incorporate the gift of giving**

  It is easy to receive, but better to give. Everything given to you, from your earthly and Heavenly Father, has been given freely. Therefore, you must give freely. While you are not expected to pay me pack or necessarily give back, you are expected to give to others and to pay it forward. All of your life, you have witnessed me giving to others and serving the community. Not only have we taken people into our home, we have regularly made certain that the needs of others have been met. Whether through clothing and shoe drives, mission trips, grocery give away, feeding programs, prison ministry or the like, it has been modeled before you to give.

  It is good, to do good. And you should do good, as often as you are able to. Not only is giving a good thing, it's a God thing and what goes around, comes back around. Whatever you sow, you will one day reap. If you sow sparingly and grudgingly you will reap the same, but if you give generously and happily, not only will you feel good about it, but goodwill comes back to you. Being selfish, is not a Sanders characteristic and nowhere in our DNA. We have a rich history of being selfless and giving back. This is who we are and this is what we do. Keep the legacy of charity and benevolence alive, as there is always someone in need and the Lord has blessed you, to be a blessing.

- ## Don't loan or co-sign

  Once you have established a good name, credit and have your financials in order...protect it at all cost. Not only should you not do anything to jeopardize what you have worked so hard for, don't allow anyone else to either. When you have been financially responsible, you have access to attain and the ability to acquire just about anything that money can buy. But because you have been listening and learning from our daddy talks, you will be wise and disciplined. But inevitably, there will be someone who didn't have the benefits of these life lessons and/ or who was not responsible with their finances. So when they attempt to make large purchases that exceed their resources and they are denied credit, there will be those that will approach you and ask you to co-sign to help them out. DON'T DO IT!

  The temptation to assist others in this way, will be very tempting and seem like the right thing to do and may appear to be a good thing. However, it usually does not turn out the way you might think it will. You are not only putting yourself in a very compromising position, but you stand the risk of damaging your relationship with such persons. In the event that they are unable to fulfill their commitment, not only are you responsible for their debt, inevitably you position yourself to be in a very awkward place with them. This is also the case when it comes to "loaning" others money. A rule of thumb that I have tried to live by, and that has worked very well for me so far, is to NOT loan what you are not able to give away. In the event that your loved one or friend is unable to pay you back, you then are not in a position to be at a loss and it helps to prevent you from falling out with them. The times that I have "given away/ loaned" money, I did so after calculating what I was ready to lose. And did so with a mindset that I may never see it again. This way, I prepared myself in the event that they reneged on our agreement. This protected me from having hard feelings toward them and ensured that I was not at a financial loss. It also taught me who and who not to assist in the future.

Money can be a relationship destroyer, as we need our hard earned resources to survive in this world and when someone seemingly takes advantage of you or takes you for granted, you might find yourself rather upset and at odds with the one you assisted. Because my resources are important to me and so is relationships, I have adopted this practice to protect both.

- **Establish an emergency fund**

The wisdom shared with me, from my great-grandmother, was sound and practical..."save something for a rainy day." Since we are unable to predict the rainy seasons in our lives, it is a good practice to incrementally put aside a portion of your resources for emergencies. It would be nice if you knew when said emergencies will occur and what is needed when they do, but life doesn't work that way. Therefore, reserve some in advance and every time you generate any kind of revenue.

Depending on whose counsel you seek, you might be told a number of things in regards to saving for an emergency fund. But what has worked for me, is to make a clear distinction between your savings and your emergency fund. As taught to you in our daddy talks, save for your future and for your golden years, but separately from that, save for true emergencies. As you establish your own household, you will have unexpected situations that will arise and can be both an inconvenience and a financial blow. Whether it is for car repair, the repair or replacement of home fixtures or appliances or for other unforeseen hardships, you will need access to resources to respond accordingly. You never know when your health may present challenges and you are out of work for extended periods of time. Neither can you predict abrupt unemployment, but you can prepare for it. By having reserved six to twelve months, or more, in an emergency fund, it will ease the burden while you are getting your leverage back. And it will keep you from exhausting your retirement savings. If all possible, never touch your savings and only access your emergency funds, in the event of a true emergency. When you budget properly, you will have discretionary resources available for things that come up, but are not emergencies. Protect your savings, investments and emergency funds and refrain from touching them, except for its intended purposes. My children, listen to me now and you will thank me later. Again, this was not taught to me and because I didn't know the difference and didn't plan accordingly, I had to play catch-up. It is better to be proactive, rather than living life in a reactionary mode. Someone has rightfully said, "if you fail to plan, you plan to fail." Don't plan to fail.

CHAPTER 4

Play Nicely

Learning interpersonal skills and how to get along with others, is essential to adulthood and success. Networking and socializing skills are imperative to surviving and thriving in today's society. We must learn how to play nicely.

• • •

One of the things that I was taught and learned early on was to not be selfish. I had to learn that being stingy was not a part of my families way of doing things and that it was expected of me to share. My mother would make it a point to intervene, when I was not playing nicely and when I kept others out of my "sandbox." I am the oldest of three and am a loner by nature. Though I love the company of others, I am most often more comfortable doing things alone. Those early years of being the only child and often left alone, caused me to develop a certain comfort level in being alone which resulted in me choosing to be alone. I found joy in my own company and was not quick to let people into my space. Though my mother didn't explicitly articulate it this way, she taught me that no man is an island and that I needed to learn to include others into my world. I must admit, I still am very reclusive and private and though I am surrounded by many loved ones and caring people, I naturally gravitate to my own corner and choose to do things alone. I have learned to be more of a people person, as my profession and activities in the community call for it. But I am not most comfortable with hob knobbing or small talk. I am a huge giver and by no means am stingy. So sharing my resources is no problem at all. But sharing my space and time...I have to work on.

I am pleasantly surprised that my children are much different than I, in this area. They make friends very easily; they know no strangers and are well liked by most. They have no problem chatting it up and socializing. It is a characteristic that I often covet, but in being honest and true to myself, I do not go out of my way to change it. Perhaps it's a character flaw or maybe just how I'm wired. I am not sure, but that is just me. I therefore have tried to be intentional in ensuring that my children do not take on my behavior. I have made it a point to remind them that their character is a gift and to use it in a positive way. I have emphasized the importance of developing and building strong interpersonal skills and to 'play nicely' when interacting with others. I am proud to say, this behavior is quite natural for them and that I do not have to spend much energy in reinforcing this to them. They are very likeable people and others find joy in their company. Nonetheless, I have deposited a few nuggets to encourage them and to ensure that they continue in this vane. Again, I am affording you an opportunity to eavesdrop on some of those daddy talks.

Daddy Talks

My children, one who desires to have friends, must first show themselves to be friendly. You all possess a quality that many, including myself, do not have. You naturally gravitate to people and vice versa. You are all leaders, in your own right and your influence is powerful. Do not take that lightly and do not minimize it. You all have talents and gifts that people enjoy watching and because of them, you are exposed to a very diverse group of people. Likewise, people desire to be a part of your world and celebrate your contributions. However, never let your abilities or popularity cause you to get the big head or to become a snob. Have confidence, but shun away from arrogance. Though you may do some things better than others, you are not better than anyone. Always be a team player and share the glory. Encourage others and be a supporter of others. Never hog the ball and learn to share the spotlight. No one likes a show off and people are turned off by people who gloat and boast. I am happy to note that this is not something that any of you have been guilty of, but I find it prudent to spend a few moments to reiterate these nuggets of wisdom.

You all have demonstrated great character when shining on your own stage and I have witnessed you time and time again, display humility and modesty. That is wonderful and makes me very proud. Continue to practice these virtues and always use your role in a positive manner. As natural born leaders, you have used your sway in ways that have charged and challenged others to give and do their best. This does not only set you a part, but will benefit you greatly in the future. Your skill set and personality stand out and brings a great deal of attention to you, to the extent that you are sought out. Use this for the greater good and look for opportunities to uplift others.

Beware, not everyone will celebrate your success and many may even find it to be offensive. Some will unfortunately use it as a means to find fault, grow jealous and may even grow to dislike you. Nonetheless, be good to others and do not use the ill-feelings of others as a license to deviate from being true to yourself and doing good. Though you might encounter negative vibes, choose to be kind and always be gracious toward others. Remember, you not only represent yourself, but you represent your family and your faith is on display. Always give grace and refrain from returning evil for evil. If people choose to not be kind toward you, you still have a responsibility to be kind toward them. When others are hateful or spiteful toward you, avoid the temptation of allowing your feelings and emotions to cause you to get out of character. You have been chosen for greatness. Be honorable and never feel like you have to stoop to low levels, just because others choose to do so. In the words of Michelle Obama, "when they go low, you go high." You gain everything when you take the high road, but you lose a lot when you go low. Do not jeopardize your potential and good standing, just because others struggle with your success. Take these words to heart and incorporate them into your everyday life. You will be the better for it and people will take note.

Though there is more that can be said, I will leave you with this. You must learn to do to others, what you want in return. You may not always get in return what you give, but still treat others in a way that you desire to be treated. It doesn't cost you much to be nice, but it can and will cost you everything when you are not nice. The law of reciprocity is real and what goes around does indeed come back around. You may not always see the immediate fruit or benefits of your actions, but trust me, they will materialize and manifest. When you do good, good comes back. Likewise, when you do evil, such will be returned. Be advised, no good deed goes unnoticed. You might not always get acknowledgment or appreciation for your actions, but you don't do good to get anything in return. Even though goodwill is eventually returned to you. Bottom line, play nicely.

CHAPTER 5

Independence Day

*Though we are created to be interdependent and have
healthy interpersonal relationships, we must also learn
to be independent. Whether we live in a single family unit
or one day choose to marry and have children, we have to
learn how to establish and maintain our own household
and prepare ourselves for independence. Therefore, there
must be a significant amount of time and effort to plan for
takeoff. Just as an eagle prepares it's eaglets for the real
world and for takeoff, we must prepare our children to
do the same. The story of how eagles parent and prepare
their young is rather fascinating. For a season, the eagle
provides; housing, food, protection and instruction. After
that season has past, the young eaglet is prepared to launch
out and care for themselves. Part of the preparation is the
once comfortable nest is made uncomfortable and instead
of the eagle hunting for and providing the daily spoil, the
young are forced to acquire nourishment for themselves.
At some point, the young are literally tossed out and forced
to fend for themselves and fly. They naturally have the
equipment to fly and are given a crash course on how to do
so. We can learn a lot from the eagles, in the preparation
for our young and in teaching them how to survive and be
successful. In our attempts to teach them to be independent,
we must teach them independent living skills.*

• • •

There will come a time when your babies will no longer be babies. And will get to the point that they need to be weaned off the nipple. For many, this is painful, but not as painful as one developing teeth and still trying to access milk and nourishment from their parental source. We are designed and wired to rely on our parents for a period of time. After which, we must be equipped to acquire nourishment for ourselves. Have you ever seen a child that has long passed the breastfeeding stage, still attached to the nipple? It is a very disturbing thing to encounter. Or even one who should be potty-trained, but still wearing pull ups? Of course I am sensitive enough to realize that various cultures and conditions influence the appropriate time to be transitioned and by no means am I being judgmental in such instances, but for the most part age and ability heavily dictates and determines when it's time to grow-up. So is the case when it comes to being independent.

There are many adolescents and adults that give evidence that they have gotten older, but have not matured. And there are many examples of adults that have not been prepared to live for themselves and live on their own. I am a parent and I get it, it's hard to let go and it's very difficult to not be the nurturing caregiver that we have become accustomed to being. But we do our offspring a great disservice, when we do not equip and empower them for independence. It is sometimes easier and sometimes second nature to just do things for them, even in their older years. Though it might be easier and second nature, it is not natural and it does them a great disservice. I have been guilty of this, myself. And as a result, I have witnessed that in my attempt to shield my children, I have sheltered my children. And because they were sheltered, there were some things that they should have been able to do on their own and or some things that they should know. But because I deprived them of learning and doing it for themselves, I crippled them and stunted their growth.

I had a very difficult upbringing and struggled growing up. There were many things that I was not privy to and certain things, materially, that I had to go without. So as an adult and as a parent, I vowed to ensure that my children didn't experience such hardships. What I didn't realize, was that my hardships actually prepared me for reality and made me a better person. I learned to appreciate the "little things" and to not take things for granted. I also learned some very invaluable lessons that made me well rounded. Me, remembering the embarrassment of the utilities being shut-off, not having the latest fashions, empty refrigerators and bare cupboards, I never wanted my children to experience that. Noble and responsible, yes, but sometimes we can go to great extremes in trying to protect and provide.

Because my children, by the grace of God, didn't have to encounter the hardships that I did, I discovered that they had developed a sense of entitlement and an unhealthy co-dependence. Something as simple as using public transportation and negotiating their way around town was foreign to them. Knowing how to maneuver and handle business for themselves was something that was always handled by mom and dad. That is great, that they were fortunate to have two loving parents that ensured their well-being was taken care of, but it deprived them of knowing how to take care of themselves, in some instances. It hindered them in learning some very key independent living and survival skills.

An eye opener for me was when my children were of age to go off to college and moved out of our nest. I had silent anxiety attacks, just at the thought of them being away and on their own. I found myself going through bouts of self-doubt and questioning if I had taught them everything that they needed to know. I feared them being out in the wild, without my immediate and easily accessible protective covering. In my attempts to make certain that they were always taken care of, I had failed in some instances, to teach them to care for themselves. There were so many things that I had planned to teach them and or just assumed they knew, but time had seemingly run out and I came to the hard realization that they were unprepared. I have to admit, I am also guilty of being blinded by my refusal to see them as aging adolescents and now adults. In my mind, they were still my little ones and my denial prevented me from noticing that they were now taller than me and had reached an age where it was time for them to transition. What a shocker it can be, when your baby is now able to go and legally order a drink. I still, to this day, cannot get use to my children having a cocktail and admittedly, fuss and growl when I witness them having libations. Of course, they quickly remind me that they are not only legally old enough, but have been for quite some time.

I personally do not think that I will ever accept this, no matter what age, but it is a reality. The first time that I saw my eldest daughter with a daiquiri, I almost blew a gasket. You would have thought that she had committed a cardinal sin. For me, it was as if she had. It was just another reminder, that they do grow up and we have no choice but to let them. We cannot stop it from happening. It is a natural part of life. Nonetheless, it revealed the difficulty in letting go and the imbalance to not be too over protective.

What helped to crystalize things for me, was the story of the dilapidated butterfly. The story is told of a little lad who had witnessed a caterpillar experiencing a metamorphosis through the process of chrysalises. While in the cocoon, he noticed that the caterpillar who was midway transitioning into a butterfly, was seemingly struggling. He, noticing the struggle decided that he would help the soon to be butterfly by breaking open the cocoon and setting the insect free. Not realizing in his attempts to help, he hurt and hindered it from blossoming and growing. As the half developed butterfly was unable to take flight and forever was grounded, as its wings were not fully developed. What he didn't realize, is that it was the "struggle" while inside the chrysalises of the cocoon that produced and pumped the necessary fluids into the wings to prepare it for flight. Because he interfered and interrupted that natural process, the insect was crippled and unable to fully develop. I, in my attempts to help my children, was guilty of hurting and hindering my children as I had become that little lad, interrupting and interfering with nature and the natural course of development. They needed to experience certain things, so that they would be strengthened and strong enough to survive on their own and reach their full potential. My foolish, though well intended efforts was actually hurting and not helping them. What a sobering and sad thing to realize and admit, but it was true.

Though, we as parents might have good intentions, it is not good to smother and shelter. I had become that parent who spent more time sheltering and smothering, rather than showing them the way. Though it was delayed, it was not too late. As I have since begun to have a series of daddy talks, centered around "preparing for take-off." Below are snippets of those talks.

Daddy Talks...

> My children, I have always wanted the very best for you. All sensible parents want the best for their children. While I may not have reached all of my goals and am by no means wealthy, yet, I've kept you safe and secured. You have always had a decent house to live in and have had all of your needs met. You have been able to experience and enjoy life, at levels of comfort that I only dreamt of. You have never known homeless or hungry nights and never went without having both parents directly involved in your upbringing. Your mother and I have always been there and you have not had to wonder who or where your father was, as he has always been in the house and involved in every aspect of your life. Unfortunately, that was not the case for me and my narrative was quite different.
>
> I had to witness a great deal, growing up and experienced quite a bit in the process. Not only did I grow up in poverty, the projects,

housing developments and a heavily crime infested inner city; I was forced to grow up rather quickly. My mother, may she rest in peace, was rather young when she had me. She had a very limited education, no career and relied heavily on government assistance. My father paid no child support, paid no attention to our needs and though he was a street hustler, we never benefited from "the spoils." He too had a limited education and no career and spent a good portion of my developing years, incarcerated. My only clear memories of his presence were occasional Sunday dinners. But let's be clear, our Sunday dinners resembled nothing close to what we experience around the dinner table on Sunday afternoons/early evenings. Sunday dinner with my mother and biological father consisted of mom cooking a big meal and instead of placing it on fine china, which we didn't have anyway, it was placed on mix-matched plastic ware and covered in aluminum foil. Then placed in a brown Safeway Foods paper bag and transported 50 miles west, to the state penitentiary.

After going through security, being patted down and waiting forever, we would then eventually be escorted to "the yard" and ate dinner amongst countless other inmates, visitors and correctional officers. I, not knowing any better and thinking this to be normal, just went along with what had become a periodic family tradition. It was about the only sense of a nuclear family that I knew and the most time I ever spent with my father. As I grew older and realized that this was not normal or natural, I vowed to change the narrative for my family. By no means would my children be forced to experience jailhouse Sunday dinners or be forced to grow up in the same milieu as I. I wanted better for you all and better is what I have tried my best to provide. It might not be the best, but trust me, it was far better than what I had to experience.

However, in my attempts to not fail you, in some regards I have. I have such deep love for you and am so grateful to be a father and in particular, your father that I may love too hard and too deep, if that was possible. My love for you and deep commitment to fatherhood is so strong, that I have possibly taken it too far or not far enough. However you choose to look at it. What I am saying to you is that I may have cuddled and coddled you a little too much. To the extent that I have not allowed you to go and grow. I know that at times you felt as if your mother and I were a little too strict and over protective. And perhaps that was true at times. Perhaps you thought that we were a little too hands on and kept you "caged." Again, maybe there is some truth to that. In my efforts to give you a different experience than I, I now realize that there is so much that you were not equipped for. Partly because you were shielded and sheltered and partly because I just flat out didn't fully or properly prepare you for independent living. I had taken great pride in always doing and always providing, that I neglected to show you the way. While you all enjoyed eating good meals and family classic dishes, we failed to give you the recipe and teach you how to make it for yourselves. While you enjoyed a lighted house, free access to running water and a temperature regulated home, we failed to tell and teach you how these things are made possible. These amenities are not just available and accessible, you have to secure services and pay for them. I was just so happy to provide the lights and water, that I didn't tell you the mechanics behind it. Instead of teaching you that your long luxury showers and baths came at a cost, so be efficient, I just paid the bill. Instead of showing you how multiple electronics and lights left on increased the monthly bill, I just paid it. Having experienced periods in my younger years where the toilet didn't flush, because the water was cut off it was my joy to prevent that from happening and save you the embarrassment of such. When candles were used to light the house, because the electricity was cut off, I just learned to adapt.

I couldn't imagine that being your regular experience and you getting use to that type of living. I was just grateful that you all didn't have to experience that type of inconvenience. However, I didn't think to use those painful childhood experiences, as occasions to prepare you for adulthood and independent living. Again, better late than never, as I am teaching you these things now through our "daddy talks".

Once you know better, you should do better. I am now making up for it. Your first business that you will ever run is called a household. You have to learn how to manage the affairs of your household, budget your household and keep it up. I know you thought that your clothes were always just magically cleaned and folded and put in its proper place. Well, guess what, your mother was the culprit. The washer and dryer and the detergent used to clean those clothes, cost. You know the refrigerator that you regularly opened and constantly ate from, well it is filled because your mother and I budgeted resources to acquire the foods that were accessible and available to you. When you are out and on your own, these are things that you have to consider and factor in. I know you thought that doing choirs were just our way of using free labor and or punishment. And at times perhaps it was, LOL. But there will come a time when you will have your own accommodations and unless you want to live in a pig sty, you will need to know how to keep your home clean and organized. Unless you plan to eat out every day, which is obviously costly, unreasonable and unrealistic, you need to learn how to cook for yourselves. You will need to plan and budget meals, so that you have enough to sustain you from day to day and throughout the month. You will need to know how to take care of your first small business, called a household, by learning how to handle your business. Short and simple, you need independent living skills, as you will one day be independent, on your on and out of our nice nest.

CHAPTER 6

The Birds and the Bees

Believe it or not, but we were not delivered from the stork and dropped off by the milk man. We are a result of an intimate and sexual encounter that took place between mommy and daddy. These tales about storks and special deliveries are of course stories told to young children to appease them, when they start asking questions at an early age. I never used them, but do understand how difficult it is to have a grown up conversation with small children. I understand age appropriateness and the "on a need to know basis" philosophy. However, some have either never even had these types of conversations and many have not had any depth of discussion with their older children. If we do not engage in this type of dialogue, not only will they be uninformed, but ill-informed. And we just might be setting them up for failure. Daddies must talk and in their talking, they must teach. Even about sex.

• • •

I'm not sure how other father's approached the sex talk and I obviously didn't have a model to refer to, when sitting down to talk with my children. Nonetheless, I remembered that as a young boy growing up, there were tons of myths and exaggerated stories floating around. And many of them sounded incredibly believable. Some things I learned were from other youth that had no idea what they were talking about. Some things were inflated accounts, from youth that presented themselves as "those in the know." Some things were just made up. And some things we just faked it and or tried to figure it out along the way. Granted, we were too young to even be experimenting and exploring, but the reality is that some of us got an early start. Of course, nothing to be proud of, but it is the truth.

I don't recall my mother ever sitting me down to have the sex talk. Maybe at most, I recall her saying "Don't bring no babies up in here." Perhaps that was her way of saying be responsible or wait to have sex. Whichever the case, there were far more questions than answers and I needed to know. I guess my curiosity won, because I, like many others, sought out on a quest to find out for myself. Looking back, retrospectively, I recognize the awkwardness in having that talk, but I also recognize the great importance, in having that talk. And to have that talk sooner than later. Of course, there are many variables that determine when the appropriate time is. But whenever that time is determined and whatever is deemed to be the right circumstances, parents must be and should be that initial voice.

If we fail to talk to our children and teach them about responsible and appropriate acts of intimacy, they will be forced to find out themselves and we cannot afford to leave it to chance or allow them to hear from unhealthy voices. Not only are there the risk of disease, that can lead to sterility, other health complications and death, but there is the risk of abuse and exploitation. There are predators and ill-intentioned people in this world and they prey upon the ill-informed and the vulnerable. We must get past our children's and our shyness and look beyond how uncomfortable it might be and realize how necessary it is. In some cases, their lives may depend upon it. From promiscuity to unhealthy acts, they stand chance of going down a dangerous path or creating a pattern of irresponsibility. Their natural proclivities and urges will one day lead them into a crash course with "fire and desire" and if they have not been prepared and equipped, they might get burned. Pun intended.

I must admit, the talk in and of itself, is rather difficult. And it is made even more difficult, when you add the awkwardness of a father talking to his daughters or a mother talking to her sons. I personally believe that it is good, when possible, for children to hear both voices and be exposed to both perspectives. Not only does this bring balance to the topic and equality to the discussion, but it helps the youth to be well-rounded. They are afforded the opportunity to hear how a woman thinks and feels, as well as how males think and approach matters.

As a father, my approach was rather different when having the male to male conversation, than when talking to my three daughters. The male to male conversation was rather straight forward and to the point. With my daughters, I centered it around an event...Father and Daughter Date Night. You will read more about that, in subsequent chapters, but in summary I took them out on their first date and had our talk. It not only made it less awkward for them and me, but made it memorable. I was also able to model for them, what healthy interactions should look like, between unwed males and females. I set the bar high enough to make certain that they had a high standard, but realistic enough to not set them up for failure or unrealistic expectations. The precedence was set and they now had a point of reference to refer to, when invited out on a date. I made it a point to share with them how precious they are and how to protect their pearls.

What I have discovered in our daddy talks is that there are dual benefits. Not only are they receiving good information from a caring and responsible adult who has their best interest at heart, but memories are being created. On top of that, the cycle of silence is being broken. Whether one has experienced fatherlessness or suffers from the impact of a voiceless father, daddy talk engagements helps to change the trajectory. It changes what has become the unfortunate normal narrative, in many households and gives children the much-needed paternal voice. I'm not suggesting that my input or approach is the end all be all, but it was what I felt led to do and was indeed far more than what I had to work with and from. I will allow you to eavesdrop on some of my nuggets, shared during my family's daddy talks, which were centered around, "the birds and the bees."

Ðaddy Talks...

My dear children, hear me and hear me well...don't be in a rush to grow up and don't be in a hurry to engage in adult behavior. And please, learn to control your sexual impulses. You will be better off and appreciative, if you listen and learn from these words. Trust me. You will inevitably get to a point when you start experiencing urges and curiosity, when it comes to the opposite sex. You will find yourself thinking and feeling like you are ready to experiment on higher levels of physical intimacy and you will THINK that your current love interest is "the one." Physical attraction and sensuality is a normal desire that we have, but we must develop discipline and exercise discernment, when choosing to act upon our passions. My advice is to take it slow and to take your time. I would ask that you practice abstinence and save yourself for the one you either give your last name to or the one to whose last name you take on. You must realize that you only have one opportunity to experience and enjoy the beauty of giving your spouse your most treasured gift. Once you give "it away" it is gone and you can never recapture it. So be careful to NOT give it away foolishly. Save it and save your relationship, by savoring "the gift."

One of the costly mistakes that many make is that they think sex is the glue that makes and keeps relationships together. They sadly discover that is not the case. As a matter of fact, if it is too soon and with the wrong person, it can and will distort and destroy the relationships. I know that cinema, TV and media portray an image of love and romance that would suggest otherwise, but please understand, what they present is for entertainment purposes and is designed to generate revenue. They capitalize off of what sells and guess what, sex sells. As sad as that might be, it is the truth. So you cannot trust the picture that they paint and you must be wise enough to not be deceived. If you allow yourself to be suckered in you will be greatly disappointed.

What many will suggest is that it is rather natural and normal to progress and matriculate through the various levels of intimacy. Insomuch, that the motif of baseball is used as an analogy. You will hear those that will try to convince you to move from base to base, until you ultimately hit a homerun. Sex is sacred and special and should not be deduced to such trivial metaphors. You will hear from some peers that will try to guilt you or shame you, if you do not score and will even resort to name calling when you propose abstinence. You will hear many that will claim, "everyone is doing it." The truth is, while there might be a lot of folk that are doing it, there are many that aren't. Choose to not be one of the "everyone" that they refer to and be one of the select crew of "waiters." Wait on it! You will thank me later.

Your body will go through different stages of development and you will notice things occurring inside of you and physically. Your curious nature will cause you to want to explore and experiment. This is one of the reasons that it is necessary for us to talk now, before you get caught up in something that you are not mature enough to handle. You are not ready for sex and until you find someone that you desire to spend the rest of your life with and actually make it official, you must refrain from going with the flow.

At your age and at this stage, you are not even fully developed and though your physical nature might hint otherwise, your emotional state and level of thinking capacity is not prepared to handle all that comes along with sexual intercourse. Whenever you're engaged in sexual acts with another person, you not only literally connect with them, but there are spiritual and emotional ties that are established. Some even refer to "soul ties". Whatever one chooses to call them, they exist and they can cause a great deal of damage. Please be wise and do not connect with someone who you are not connected to.

Sex is a beautiful and a wonderful gift, when practiced within a certain and sacred context. It is used for procreation, recreation and relaxation. You are able to bond with the one that you have decided to grow old with and will reach depths unimaginable and unattainable, by any other means of connection. Through it, you can partake and participate in the joy of creating and bringing about life. And there is also great pleasure and even health benefits from the union. So when the time and circumstances are right, enjoy from the gift of physical and sexual intimacy, but only when the time and circumstances are right. And when the two occur:

- **Be responsible in your sexual encounters**

  You have a responsibility at all times, to be responsible. And in your sexual interactions, you are not exempt from such. It has already been emphasized and my sentiments have been echoed repeatedly, but again I say, sex is reserved for committed couples and couples that have officially made their matrimonial bonds to one another. I know the day and age in which we live; I realize that not everyone ends up married and I realize that not everyone holds to these seemingly archaic standards. But the collateral damage that occurs is not merely a means to spiritual discipline or exercise; rather it is to protect and to preserve. Protect you from unnecessary hurts and hiccups and to preserve your essence for the one that you entrust your life to.

  While my teachings and my expectations encourage you to wait and to only engage within a certain context, I am not naïve to believe that everyone adheres to such admonishments. I hope that you do, but in the instance that you might decide to deviate from my guide, protect yourself. Protect yourself from sexually transmitted diseases, protect yourself from creating life without being positioned and prepared to care properly for that life and protect yourself from a life of reckless sexual encounters.

Once you have experimented with and experienced sex, there will be the natural desire to want to again. And if you choose to do so as a sport or for recreational purposes only, you could very easily find yourself engaging in reckless behavior. Sex is so pleasing and so powerful, it can become addictive. And there are many who have found themselves developing addictions and their proclivity is so strong and wild, that they can't get enough and in some instances their appetite is never satisfied. These types of persons oftentimes find themselves creating and fulfilling fantasy acts and even indulge in activities that involve multiple partners, at the same time. Like drugs, they build up a tolerance and are constantly looking to top the last high. Please do not let this become your narrative and heavens forbid, do not entertain pornography or other sexual exploits. I know that this talk is rather raw and may be beyond PG-13, but I cannot leave your exposure to this important topic to chance. I'd rather keep it 100 and ensure that you get the nuts and bolts from me, than from someone with slick motives who is trying to manipulate you and the situation. It is ok to say no and please know, that No means NO. Don't be afraid or pressured to not say no and if you are told no, do not press. Best you hear it straight from daddy's mouth. Be responsible.

- **Be respectful in your sexual encounters**

Not only must you be responsible, you must be respectful. As already mentioned, sex is a sacred and special act and when engaging in it, you must be respectful to your partner. You should never expose them to or expect them to do things that they are not comfortable with. And so goes the same for them to you. Both parties must be willing and in agreement and each other's wishes and comfort level must be respected. One of the side effects of pornography, sexual exploits and multiple partners is that persons can very easily develop cravings for encounters that are not normal or natural, within the confounds of a monogamous relationship. And not only can they develop desires, they can begin to make demands from the other partner. In addition to them developing deep desires and making demands, when one's special needs are not met, they can become quickly disappointed. Even to the point where they become dismissive and disregarding to their partner. And the acts can become rather deviant, one can become disrespectful and before you know it, the relationship is distorted or destroyed.

Your love interest is a human being, not a toy or an object. They must be regarded at all times and their feelings must be considered. They must be respected and the relationship must be respectful. When you begin to introduce additional sex partners and/or sexual deviance into the equation, you are playing with fire and you are not being respectful to your partner. With extracurricular sexual exposure, you may experience some things that your partner is not able to fulfill and it can create regret, insecurities and unhealthy practices. Bottom line, be respectful.

- ## Be intentional in your sexual encounters

It is equally important to be intentional. I have covered this already, but let me throw this nugget in. When you have discovered and found "the one" for you, there is a level of euphoria that is second to none. You will experience a depth and a high, like no other. Why? Because when the right type have connected, found their chemistry and unveil their compatibility, the relationship is enriched and the two reach levels of enjoyment that is unexplainable. The best intimacy is when the two are truly into one another. And because of the emotional, spiritual and mental ties that are established during intimate acts, it behooves you to be intentional in your sexual encounters. Especially when you have decided, to procreate. You must be careful with whom you decide to create life with. Your child will be a product of the two of you and if that be the case, what will you produce? A child cannot choose which family they are born into, but the parents can choose what family the child is born into and what type of family that they will be raised in. Your intentionality is imperative, because your encounters must be calculated and not careless or callous. You choose your partners, therefore, you must choose wisely. Be intentional!

CHAPTER 7

Like Father Like Son

An apple doesn't fall far from the tree. No greater joy comes to a father, than to see his seed blossom and one day become a man. And it is made complete, when he too becomes a father...

• • •

When the doctor uttered those magical words, "it's a boy," a surge of excitement rushed all throughout my body and I felt accomplished and invincible. The joy of having a boy of my own and that would become my namesake, was an indescribable joy. It was a feeling that I do not think I could ever fully explain. To say that I was happy, indeed is an understatement. I always dreamt of having a boy. I envisioned playing catch, wrestling around on the living room floor, shooting baskets and hearing a tenor/bass version of, "Dad!" And when this happened, I thought that I had arrived.

I am fortunate to be a father to both genders and each have deposited into my joy tank a sense of fulfillment that has made me feel a sense of wholeness that pales in comparison to anything else. But seeing your male seed be raised up and rise up to manhood is something that words alone are unable to capture or adequately convey. In your son, you see a reflection of yourself. And it gives you a glimpse of the younger you. If you care to give considerable thought to it, you are able to bask in the awesomeness of righting your wrongs and redirecting him, as you advise him of the many pitfalls that you fell into. You are able to give him a context and help him to map out a life that is filled with cheat-sheets and lessons that gives him an advantage. The father has already given of himself in creating and giving life to a male who by nature, takes after him. But he also gives of himself by pouring into him life experience, from a male perspective. And it is a perspective that has a sense of familiarity and familial roots that makes it that much more rewarding. This is awesome to witness and an honor to be a part of.

For almost three decades, I have heard; dad, daddy, daddio, dada, pop pops and father a million times over. This of course is collectively from all of my children and I never grow weary of hearing it. And I can honestly say that it still warms my heart and brings an incredible smile to my face when anyone of these versions is uttered. I truly love being a father and would not exchange it for anything in the world. The joy I get in knowing that I was responsible for giving and molding life is unparalleled to anything else that I have ever experienced. And though I do not have nor display greater value over one gender than the other, there is a distinct difference in rearing a son. There are certain things that you pass on to them, as a father, that are unique and tailored to the male exchange. And in this, there is great mystique and magic. I would imagine that a similar exchange takes place between that of a mother and daughter, but of course I can only speak from the male experience. And that experience is majestic.

In my adult years, I had a friend and father figure that emerged and who was responsible in shaping and molding my professional life. As a mentor, he molded me on how to conduct business helped to sharpen my business etiquette and coached me on my business acumen. He also modeled for me, how to manage my manhood. Interesting enough, at this point in my life, I was not looking for a father figure nor was I seeking a malefactor to fill the void that was left throughout my childhood. However, his presence helped in ways that influenced my parenting and revealed to me the power of parenting by proxy.

Though he did not directly teach me how to parent or try to parent me, I learned a great deal by watching him. As a mentor, he would often tell me to watch him. As he conducted business and interacted with the community, his counsel to me was "pay attention and watch." And that's what I did. I watched. Not only was I able to learn from his professionalism, I learned from his parenting. It was not something that he sought out to teach, but because I was paying attention and watching, I was able to pick up and learn things that transferred over to my parenting.

This experience helped me to realize something very important in my role as a father. There is power in the voice of the father and there is power in the presence of the father. What was obvious is that when a father is present, the child learns by; looking and when a father is present they learn by listening. And when they are looking and listening, they learn how to; lead, live and love. Lucky for me, I was good at listening and looking. I am like a sponge and soak up everything. And indeed that is what I did, I absorbed as much as I could as often as I could. And not only did it directly benefit me; it has now benefited my children and will benefit my children's children as well.

Though our relationship started off as a mere mentor to mentee, it evolved into a friendship, which evolved into an employer to employee relationship and interesting enough, we are now colleagues. Even though our relationship is multi-faceted, there were always clear lines of demarcation that never blurred and were never crossed. There was an understanding and a high level of respect that kept the sectors of our relationship separate. For the average person, perhaps it would have been complicated and confusing. But in our interaction, it worked just fine. Our friendship never interfered with our work relationship and as a colleague he was still able to mentor me without there being any conflict.

I would say that one of the reasons that this worked so well and was seemingly flawless is because of the deep respect that I had for him and because of the clarity of the segmented relationship. But I would also say, it was because of the value and importance of the relationship. Because I valued it and deemed it important, I had no problem in knowing and staying in my place. Had I not, it would have ruined the relationship and I would not be the benefactor.

I share all of this because I think that it is important to note, sons need permission for access into their father's life and it is possible to establish a multifaceted relationship, where the lines of respect and honor are not crossed or violated. I was able to experience this with my friend-mentor and therefore had now been given a prototype to use in my own father-son relationship. A mistake that many parents make is choosing to befriend their children at the risk of sacrificing parenthood. And many will trade in their parental card for a friendship card and usually the results are disastrous. Our children need us to be their parent, but it is possible to have a good friendship, if the lines of demarcation exist. I have sought to find the balance and would like to think that I have done a fairly good job in managing both aspects. I have discovered that during those unique moments of "fathering and friending," that those young eyes are watching intensely and those ears perk up, even when you are not aware. They are looking and listening and paying close attention to everything that you say, do and even to the things that you do not say or do not do. All eyes are on you. And fathers, the fruit doesn't fall far. So be mindful of what you say and share.

I never really had facial hair, but in between haircuts it was necessary to shape up and shave occasional stubble. My youngest son would often walk into the restroom when I was trying to rid my face of the unwanted hair stubs and would watch me apply shaving cream and use the razor. Even though he obviously didn't have a need to shave, he would mimic my moves and copy my actions. He would

66

put the shaving cream on his face and use the stem of his toothbrush to "shave." It dawned on me that one day he may need to shave and therefore needed to learn how to do so properly. And it was my job to teach him. The funny thing is, I didn't really know how to shave either and had never witnessed or watched another practice this form of hygiene and maintenance. Nevertheless, I needed to advise him. I went through the motions and at the end, the stubble was gone. But I was ignorant to the science or technique. I assumed I was doing it right because I watched the commercials and I got the results. Because of this, I was forced to find out so that I could share the right information. Simple little principles like; don't cut against the grain, never use a dull or broken blade, lather up before shaving and use alcohol or after shave once you're done were tidbits that proved to be beneficial to the shaving experience. Yes, some things we eventually figure out, but it is helpful to have someone that can coach and advise us along the way. That is what fathers do and that is another reason why it is important to have a father in the house. As a live-in coach, children have access to counsel and greatly benefit from their experience and expertise.

This had become a far too familiar narrative that would play over, again and again. One where I would be called upon and where I would be expected to teach something that had not been taught to me. And one where I needed to model something that hadn't been modeled before me. I didn't have anyone to listen to or look at, but my seed did. Therefore I needed to make certain that I had something to say and something to share. This is where I benefited the most, from parenting by proxy. As a child and as an adult, I was afforded the opportunity to glean from the experience of others, as I was exposed to other father-son interactions.

As a child growing up, on occasion I would run across a friend that had a live-in father. And not just fathers who took up a temporary abode, but who were engaged and active in their children's lives. When I was around them, I saw what I was missing and I saw what things were supposed to look like. I looked at what they did and listened to what they said and as a result, I learned. I paid attention to the playful moments and I also paid attention to the times of discipline and correction. I heard the love in the voice of the father, as they would speak life into my friend's life and I heard the stern directness, when there was a need to redirect. I must admit, that the strength in their voice caused me to evaluate my behavior and I would make subtle changes, even though they were obviously not my father nor were they talking to me.

I had one set of friends, all male, who had one of the coolest fathers I had ever met. They all resembled him and their mannerisms were almost identical to his. They all had a certain swag and demeanor, whereby you automatically knew that there was a blood relationship. When they were all together, it was one of the most remarkable things to see. I secretly would visit, not to see my friends, but to see and be a part of this father-son exchange. While I greatly appreciated being an honorary member of the clan, I would secretly wish that I were a permanent member or at least that I could be a fly on the wall and bear witness to what life was like outside of those stolen and temporal moments. Those moments were memorable and meaningful and I paid close attention. I looked and I listened and as a result, I learned. Even though this was many years ago, I refer to those occasions and have incorporated them into my own father-son interactions. Sometimes all you have is an experience vicariously and/or by proxy. In either case, it benefited me and in turn has benefited my family.

Likewise, as an adult, I from time to time witnessed other fathers interact with their sons and I paid close attention to what they did and what they said. I didn't realize it then, but in both instances I was learning to parent by proxy. And from both experiences, I borrowed tips and tools that I would later use in my parental exchange. There were some things that I was doing that I changed, because I saw another father do it differently. This included my speech, as well as my conduct. Interesting enough, this was also true when it came to being a husband. While I thought that I was pretty decent in how I treated women and how I interacted with my wife, I would from time to time witness how other husbands did things and I would make the necessary adjustments in my husband-wife relationship. My point is that there is great power in observation. Just as I learned by looking and listening to other fathers, I realized that there are other fathers that are looking and listening to me. Most importantly, I have young male eyes that are looking and listening and learning. Learning how to live, lead and how to love.

Our sons learn how to live, by watching how we live...

Our children and in particular our sons, benefit greatly when there is a father present. They benefit sometimes through direct instruction and explicit tutelage. They also benefit from instruction that is more indirect and implicit. Some things are taught to them, because the father is intentional in sitting their young down and having sessions of impartation. These direct encounters are much needed, as the child is afforded an opportunity to engage in dialogue. Even when the exchange is more of a monologue and the youth is not able to express themselves through verbal articulation, they still benefit from thoughtful guidance of the father. These moments are priceless, as they create memories as well as playbook for the child to playback and refer to.

Teaching our children how to tie their shoe is one example of direct and explicit instruction, but a son discovering that dad doesn't use the restroom by sitting down like mommy is an indirect implicit example of teaching. My youngest son one day decided that he would demonstrate his manhood and growth, by using the restroom on his own and without alerting anyone. He was no longer satisfied with sitting on his child-size potty; he felt it was time for him to use the big-boy potty. Being proud of himself and feeling accomplished, he uttered out "Look, I'm using the bathroom like daddy." He was learning by looking, even when I didn't realize it and it of course created the opportunity for me to teach him how to handle his business. Our sons learn how to live, by watching how we live and negotiate around the house. They want to be like daddy. They want to wear daddy's smell goods, walk in daddy's shoes and play with daddy's ties. Even though I would buy multiple wave brushes, picks and deodorants, somehow some way mine was always used. I guess there was just something about sharing dad's stuff and wanting to do things like dad. My flow around the house was being watched and played out. Some of those things were good and some were not so good. Our sons will pick up on certain things that appeal to them and they will incorporate them into their lives. The father's movement around the house will give a template for our sons, on how to live. The father's demeanor and disposition in how he handles family and household affairs, is being watched. The father going to work or not going to work, daily, is being watched. How the father dresses, how he interacts with others and how the father deals with life overall, is being watched. Our sons are looking and listening and they are learning how to live, based upon how the father lives.

Our sons learn how to lead, by watching how we lead...

Our sons learn how to lead, as they watch the father lead. How the father leads the family, leads in his work ethics, leads in household management and how he leads in parenting has a huge impact on how his children will lead. In some instances, the child will despise how the father leads and lives and will want no parts of it. They will shun away from the example set and will create a model that is contrary. While in most cases they will mirror what was demonstrated and portrayed before them. In either case, it is important and imperative to know and note that fathers have a great influence on how their sons lead, based upon how they themselves lead.

I do feel it necessary, to acknowledge the fact there are some fathers that lead effectively from within the home and some that lead effectively outside of the home. While I advocate, when all possible, that fathers remain in the home and lead from within, I do have sense enough to know that not all family dynamics are the same and that this is not always ideal or possible. However, the father not being present in the house does not mean that he cannot have an impact on the household. Every family situation is different, so there is no cookie cutter approach that works for all. What I am saying though, is a father can have significant sway and say even though they do not live in the same household. They may be absent from the family home, but they can be present in the family's affairs. Again, I recognize some families have complicating scenarios and that there are variables that prevent smooth co-parenting. The fact still remains, in most situations fathers still have input.

I've witnessed split relationships where the couple has made a conscious decision to not allow their broken relationship to impact the relationship of their child. They put the child first and chose to co-parent and though the father may not "run" the house that he is not living in, he is able to lead in that house and the co-parenting experience. How this plays out will vary from house to house, family to family and from situation to situation. Nonetheless, be mindful that our sons learn to lead by looking and listening to how we lead.

Our sons learn how to love, by watching how we love...

While I did have the fortunate opportunity to tell and teach how a man should treat a lady, what spoke louder than my voice was my actions. Because our household included both parental influences, the interaction between my wife and I were observed on a daily basis.

My children were learning how to love and learning how to be loved, by the opposite sex. As our sons are looking and listening, fathers, they are learning to love and engage in the male-female exchange. They learn basic etiquette and respect, when interacting with women. They learn how to be sensitive and considerate and caring. They learn how to listen to women and how to be in tune and show interest. They learn the importance of and how to affirm and validate. They learn how to love, by watching how their father loves. In all of this, we must be aware that they most likely will mimic and mirror what is modeled before them. Therefore, be mindful to what is modeled and be intentional on how you mold them.

Though there is great joy and fulfillment for a father to have a son, being a father is incomplete, if the son is not a positive reflection of the father. This is of course my opinion. I am not merely talking about having a physical resemblance, but a true authentic reflection of who you are as a person. They reflect your morals, ethics and values. While everyone is different and will eventually develop their own philosophies in life, we reproduce ourselves through our children. We pass on foundational trues that should help to shape and sharpen them, as they grow. They will one day develop and discover their own path, but for the most part they should reflect what they have been exposed to. I believe this to be true physically and spiritually as well as genetically.

I recall going to the doctor's office for a routine visit. They wanted to do a wellness check and began to ask me a bunch of questions. They not only asked questions about my family on my mother's side, but dug deep and began to interrogate me about family health conditions on my father's side. I have to sadly admit, that I sat there with a rather perplexed look on my face. I didn't know how old my father was, didn't know his date of birth, I knew of no medical history for him or anyone on his side of the family. I was totally clueless and couldn't answer any of his questions. The doctor was not attempting to embarrass me, of course, but was trying to build a medical profile and discern if there were any health trends to watch for or any genetic abnormalities that we needed to be aware of. Nonetheless, I had no information to give and the questionnaire they gave me was virtually blank.

This type of information is key as some of us are genetically predisposed to certain illnesses and disease that could be treated in a proactive manner, rather than reactively. The sooner that you are aware of your family history, the better your chances at treating a problem. Just as we can and do carry on health genes from our parents, we too carry on traits and mannerisms. Some are learned and others are passed on through our DNA. My point is two-fold; knowing your father not only helps you to know yourself better, but provides a baseline and explanation for some of your behaviors. And as certain things are passed on from one generation to the next, we are able to get a glimpse of excerpts from those who precede us. In some regards, we relive the lives of our ancestors and some things are repeated. In knowing your father, it helps you to know more about yourself.

While in some regards we do repeat things from previous generations, it is rather unhealthy, when parents or grandparents attempt to live vicariously through the lives of their offspring and or impose their unfulfilled lives upon them. As a result, they pass on unrealistic expectations and make demands that are unfair, depriving their children an opportunity at discovering and living life for themselves. For some parents, who live with regret of failure, they hijack the lives of their young and dictate what path they should take and superimpose their wishes and desires. They determine what career path is best and even go as far as interjecting their opinions in the selection of a mate for their children.

Not only is it unfair, to force your unfulfilled life upon your child, it is unnatural. True the fruit doesn't fall far from the tree, but everyone is entitled to live their own life and to tailor it to their own personal design. Unfortunately, too many have been robbed of this treasure and as a result have lived miserable lives, filled with deep remorse and regret. Admittedly, it can be very helpful to have a parent guide you, but it is not healthy when the parent decides for you. There is indeed great honor when a child continues the family legacy, by either taking on the same or a similar career path as their parent or when they take over the family business. But it can be horrible, when there is not a natural desire to do so, and instead it is forced upon them.

The idiom, "the apple doesn't fall far from the tree" is very true and our children are indeed a reflection of their parents and a result of their parenting. This being the case, we as parents and in particular fathers, must be careful at what we produce.

CHAPTER 8

Daddy's Girls

A daughter's first encounter and experience with the opposite sex should be by and with her father. He should model for her, how a man is to treat a woman and demonstrate proper and healthy interactions. I took my daughters out on their first date and gave them a promise ring...

• • •

Father and Daughter First Date

S everal years ago, I took my eldest daughter out on her first date, one by one and at different times/ages. I was so excited and couldn't wait for her to turn 16. My philosophy is that I want to be the first one to take my daughters out and in doing so I hope to model for them how they are supposed to be treated.

Sydney Ra'Chelle, my eldest daughter, and I went out to dinner to a restaurant of her choosing. She wanted Red Lobster and that is where we went. Afterwards, we went to a very popular and somewhat historic and touristic area in our home town, the Old Market. There, we walked and talked and just enjoyed one another's company. The Old Market tour was incomplete, without a horse and buggy ride. Never did I imagine that such an outing with my daughter could be so much fun. I later took her back home and I modeled how a night out is supposed to end. She went to her room and I went to mine.

During dinner that evening, I gave her a promise ring and shared with her that as long as she wore that ring, she was to be reminded of her promise. The ring is not to come off, until it is replaced by a competent suitor who must approach me for permission to remove MY ring. In removing and replacing MY ring, he is agreeing to take over where I left off. These basic expectations of course are centered around him caring for her and taking care of her.

I truly enjoyed my night out, with my eldest princess and hoped that she would forever remember our special occasion. I later asked her to recap her thoughts of the evening and her experience and she said something that blew me away. She said that she felt so special and that she never wanted that moment to end. She recalls that she was sad, when the night had to end, because she didn't want it to be over. That not only brought tears to my eyes, but was flattering. That someone thought so much of an encounter that they did not want the moment to ever end. WOW! I love you Syd and will always replay that moment, in my mind.

Desiree' Monique, my middle daughter, accompanied me for our first date at age 14. I took Sydney out at 16, but decided to take Desiree' out at 14 because the fast paced and developing youth culture, demanded earlier intervention. Desiree' chose to go to Red Lobster as well. Prior to our first date, neither had been to Red Lobster, so it was special to them. After dinner, we went to a Broadway Musical, The Color Purple. It was awesome!!! We had a great time and she too stated that she didn't want it to end. She said that she felt like a princess. That being said, one of my objectives had been accomplished. I continuously remind all three of my daughters that they are my princesses and I truly hoped they really believed it. The comment that night seemed to indicate so.

Sunday, September 22, 2014 my last and youngest baby and I went on our date. We went to Kobi's Japanese and Steakhouse and to the Old Market for a horse and buggy ride. I had promised her a full day at the spa, but since homecoming was the following weekend, we decided to wait on the spa until the day before homecoming.

I purchased all of them a "promise ring/purity ring." The ring was placed on their left ring finger, as a symbol of me being their covering, until another comes to take over. As their covering, I am responsible for their wellbeing; spiritually, emotionally, physically, financially and mentally. The person that desires to replace my ring has to be willing and able to take full responsibility to care for them, as I have. This is critical. If he is not concerned about her whole being, then he needs not even waste his time. Once she leaves my covering, she is no longer my responsibility and therefore, the man that enters into her life must understand what he is getting into and be able to handle it. The ring is to also serve as a symbol of our covenant, a reminder of our covenant and reinforcement that as long as the ring is on, they are to adhere to our covenant.

As a promise ring, it is to remind them of the promise that they made before me and their promise made before God. They were promising to remember the lessons taught, from our daddy talks and throughout their upbringing. They were promising to be committed to a life of purpose and to strive to reach their full potential. They were promising to apply themselves, never sell themselves short and never to forget who they are. The ring was a reminder of the promise to forever remain true to themselves and to show honor to their name and family lineage.

The ring also served as a purity ring. As such, they were agreeing to remain pure, by remaining abstinent. They were accepting the challenge to wait for a suitable suitor to remove and replace MY ring, with their own. It would be then and then only, that they would give themselves in the most intimate way that two human beings can. After wedding, they would be released to share the great gift that they treasured, with the one that proved themselves to be worthy. Though this almost sounded cliché and liken to a fairy tale, I thought it to be rather realistic and a reasonable standard. Not everyone adheres to such standards, but it is better to at least have one. Of course the ring is to never be removed, unless it's being replaced. That being the case, as long as it is on, they are charged to REMEMBER what it means and what it is for.

There are nine principles that I was certain to cover, on our date. These principles are very basic and do not boast to be conclusive or exhaustive. There are other things that we have and will discuss, but for the purposes of our date, these thoughts surfaced and were shared. These nine practical principles and talking points are:

1. **Remember what you have seen.** Dad has set the precedence and you should not go backwards when entertaining your potential love interest. Since their early childhood, I have attempted to affirm them, love them, cherish them, care for them, provide for them and treat them with dignity. I talk to them a certain way and I treat them a certain way. I do not degrade them, devalue them or dehumanize them. This has not only molded them, but has been modeled before them. And in doing so, precedence has been set. They know how their daddy has treated them therefore no "lil jackleg" can come to them sideways. They now have a point of reference to compare their current treatment to. Their father doesn't call them out of their name, so they should not allow anyone else to either. Their dad treats them with dignity; therefore any male that comes into the picture must do the same. If they cannot or will not at least start there, they can keep it moving. I cannot say that I have done everything right, but I have at least attempted to be a positive model and in the process, molded them into young ladies who knew the difference between a prince and a jester.

2. **Remember what you have been taught.** With the precedence being set, a standard is being formed. And it is up to them,

to set that standard. Now that I have set the precedence and groomed them, they must begin to build upon that and establish standards that match up with this precedence. A person without standards is a person that is most likely to go for and settle for anything. Once standards have been set, a person has a starting point that they can either choose to lower or set higher. This is the baseline and ground level. The bare minimum is for courtesy and mutual respect. Of course the desire is that the standards would never be lowered or compromised. In setting these basic standards, I expect them to:

(A) Set Boundaries;

(B) Have Expectations and;

(C) Maintain Respect for self and others.

3. **The setting of boundaries.** I have taught my daughters the importance of establishing comfort and privacy zones. These have become a set of perimeters that should never be encroached upon or violated. No one should enter your comfort or privacy zones, unless invited. This was important to share, because sometimes the lines are blurred when it comes to our instructions and expectations to our children in the adult child relationship. Allow me to explain. We teach our children to not talk back or disrespect adults. We teach them to follow instructions and not to be disobedient to adults. And this is good and sound teaching. However, what is sometimes omitted is, when there should be exceptions to that rule. So many children are exposed to folk who are not pure in their intentions and use their role as an adult, to manipulate the child and take advantage of them and their innocence. I suggest that at an early age, parents and in particular fathers, begin to have those talks about setting boundaries. And in doing so, it is not a bad idea to teach

them who the safe adults are and under what circumstances that even the safe adults should be permitted to near such zones. I am suggesting that they be taught that anyone attempting to encroach beyond those boundaries, that they ask permission and explain why it is necessary to enter into these personal zones. They should be empowered to say NO, if they do not feel comfortable and not be instructed to just allow people to say or do anything to them, just because they are an adult. Therefore, boundaries must be set and not violated or compromised.

4. **Have Expectations.** If you expect nothing, chances are that's exactly what you will get. Of course there are exceptions to the rule and instances where this could be debated. But I think that most get the spirit of this statement. You should always have expectations for yourself and expectations from those that you choose to interact with. You ought to know beforehand, what you desire and seek from your union and how it and they can contribute to your overall life quest. Because you have standards and a precedence has been set, you should expect to be treated a certain way and addressed a certain way. You should expect to be respected and your reasonable wishes be honored. Because you do not have time to waste and time is precious, never allow anyone to take advantage of your time. Don't be afraid to ask, where is this going? Don't be afraid to back out or away, if it and they are not going in the same direction as you. It's better to get off a bus going in the wrong direction, than to stay on a bus that will take you somewhere you are not supposed to be. Some might suggest that if you don't have expectations, then you will never be disappointed. When in actuality, the opposite is true. When you do not have expectations, you are most often painfully surprised rather than pleasantly surprised. To not have expectations is liken to going on a road trip without any

sense of directions or without a set of directions. Not only do you not have any idea where you are going, which way you should travel or how long it will take, chances are you will end up lost and frustrated.

5. **Maintain Respect for self and others.** Not only should you demand that others have respect for you, it is a virtue to ensure that you have and show respect to yourself and others. Never compromise others and never allow others to challenge you to compromise. Your integrity is priceless and should never be diluted. You must be a person who is sensitive to others and take into consideration how your actions will and could affect them.

6. **Be self-reliant and carry your own weight.** Don't expect or demand anyone to do anything for you. And the only time that you should put your hand out, is when you need a hand up. Only when you are truly in need, should you rely upon others. Otherwise, learn to do for yourself. Be prepared to carry your own weight. One tragic mistake that is often made is ambiguous agreements, expectations and/or arrangements. The female can come across as a "gold-digger" that expects the man to "do for her" and the male can come across as having ulterior motives, who expects or demands something in return. I have taught my daughters to:

(A) Be prepared to cover their expenses;

(B) Be prepared to seek and/or attain alternate transportation, if the outing goes south;

(C). Be in a position to always be able to make an emergency call, if necessary;

(D). Always be alert and plan for and expect the unexpected!!!!

7. **Never sell out or sell yourself short.** Do not feel obligated to oblige or made to feel indebted. I have taught you and made it inexplicably clear, just because he buys you a happy meal, does not mean you have to make him "happy." And just because he may have paid for the night of entertainment, does not mean you have to "entertain" him. That way if you sense an indication that there are expectations, you are prepared to cover your own expenses and execute an exit strategy. Remember, daddy is only a phone call away.

8. **Listen with your eyes and ears.** Conversation is critical. Be certain the night includes opportunity for unhindered conversation. I have taught you to discern his true character, by attentively listening to what he talks about. Strategic conversation discloses a great deal about a person. You can learn a lot, if you simply have a conversation and are good at listening. What is he talking about? Who is he talking about? What is he NOT talking about? etc...

   His respect toward others gives you a glimpse of how respectable he is as an individual and how respectful he may be towards you. I have taught them to observe how he treats them, refers to them and how he treats and refers to others. If out to eat, how does he interact with the public and/ or wait staff. Is he on his phone with other people; texting or chatting? Is his attention on you or on everyone and everything else? All of this gives insight into who he really is and how he really acts. Of course folk can snowball you at first, but if you truly pay attention, you can see the red flags.

9. **Practice Modesty.** He should return you in the same physical condition in which he found you. My daughters have been taught and warned, when you come back to MY HOUSE, there better not be any indication or insinuation of "foul play." During our date out, it was modeled for them to be

home at a decent hour and the date ended with them going to their respective room and me going to mine. Dessert was included with dinner! There is no such thing as a nightcap or "capping the night off." Not on my watch.

Of course there is a lot more that has been taught and a great deal still to be taught/modeled. However, these are some of the basics and I just pray that my daughters will adhere to them. Even if they veer away from them, at least they have been taught and they will be educated on how to interact with the opposite gender. When it's all said and done, they still have the power to choose. Prayerfully, this will assist them in making the right choice. If not, my guns are loaded :-) No seriously, my guns are loaded!

While I realize that some may disagree with my philosophy, some may differ in the approach and some may even disapprove all together. One thing is for certain and that cannot be debated is that my efforts made a noticeable difference and was a defining moment in their lives. They will never forget it, nor will I and if they apply and incorporate what was shared and experienced, they will definitely benefit.

These encounters and daddy-led discussions are multi-faceted and produce incalculable results. The benefits are immeasurable and the fruit is abundant. And this initiative not only made a memorable impression upon my daughters, but on the lives of others as well. Not only have others followed suit and replicated this model, but I have been asked to fill in the gap for fathers who couldn't or wouldn't take the time to create this memory. To be clear, I am very selective and careful when doing so. And I have used strong discrimination, when agreeing to do so. And I have only accepted to do so, for family and a close friend. I take time to make this clear and to give strong caution; as well intended acts can sometimes be misconstrued, misinterpreted and mismanaged.

Some collateral damage can be avoided if choices are well calculated and deep consideration is given when making those choices. In this instance, while their might be young ladies that do not have the benefit of having their biological father in their lives, the fact is that they do have a father. Whether he is inactive or absent, he still exists. And another man coming in and playing daddy to a child that is not his can create some hard feelings and turn what was meant to be pure and innocent into an awkward moment filled with tension and rampant emotions. Especially when the excited youth relates to the surrogate father figure better than their own father.

In the early years of my working with youth, I learned hard, yet valuable lessons. Everyone does not know your heart, everyone does not know your intentions and everyone is not crazy about you "showing them up." I had a co-hort of youth that gravitated to my work and seemed to truly appreciate my involvement in their lives. Insomuch, that some of them began to refer to me as dad. While I didn't feel comfortable with them referring to me as such, I must admit it was most flattering to know that they thought so much of me and our relationship that they would bestow upon me such a coveted title. Me, anticipating the fallout by their parents, would correct them and would instruct them from refraining to me as such. Though they most often followed my instructions any other time, in this instance they often disobeyed. For them, it was a term of endearment and an expression of their deep sentiments. And for many of them, I probably was more of a father to them than their own father. Nonetheless, I was not their father and I made it painfully clear as such. As you could imagine, some fathers and even mothers took offense, and rightfully so. What they didn't realize, is that this was not my doing and I discouraged and instructed the youth to not do so. However, they felt the closeness and continued to do so. One thing that it taught me is that in the absence of a parental influence, youth will seek out and secure someone or something to fill the void. For them, I had become that someone. And our connection had become that fill to that void.

This fueled my desire to ensure that my own children had what I did not and it was my quest to be the best father that I knew to be, to and for my own children. And I discovered that this meant more than just being daddy, but included "fathering." For the purposes of this book, I have coined the term fathering and defined it as "personalized parenting that goes beyond basic parental care." What I mean by that is there are some things that you must do and will do, simply because you're a parent. And for me, that is called parenting and being a father or mother. But when you take the time to discover unique characteristics about your child and/or do things that may be considered outside of the traditional scope of things, to include being creative and at the risk of being viewed as silly, that is fathering.

Example, my daughters love to dance and are all very gifted in this area. In an attempt to connect with them and become more than their provider and protector, I got out of my comfort zone and created moments and memories where I was allowed to be free and be me. Moments that allowed them to see me in a different light and a different role from what they were accustomed to. We created dance and rap routines and even created some videos where we were intentional in acts of being silly and simply just having fun. I chose to participate in my daughter's dance recitals and not only were they blow away at me agreeing to do so, but they were tickled pink that dad actually could move. They quickly realized where their passion and gift in dance came from. I was able to channel moves from my previous life as a break-dancer and walked away leaving an indelible impression that they would never forget. For me, that's fathering.

To be in a spot where I was not the disciplinary or the parent who lorded over them to ensure that every move is monitored and measured. It was refreshing and created an opportunity for fathering. They got to see me as a human being and as an adult who knew how to have fun and that desired to have fun with them. I had learned in my early youth days that you have to earn the right to be heard.

Granted, I was dad and they had to listen, but when I intentionally chose activities that were fun and innovative and meant something to them, they wanted to listen. I had tapped into effective youth worker strategies and met them where they were. I believe that has significantly contributed to my level of effectiveness in the parental exchange. It has enhanced our relationship and not only has it broken the cycle of what they and I perceived as parenting, but it broke the silence that is evident in the paternal exchange.

One last example of this was my middle daughter being stood up and canceled on for school prom. Not only were her feelings hurt, but she was devastated as she was looking forward to this big event. She had secured her attire and made plans to ensure that she looked good and would have fun. After receiving the bad news, that she no longer had a date, she considered not attending at all. I took a chance and asked to be her date. Being a person that doesn't deal well with rejection and assuming that she would consider the thought to be lame, I was hesitant in asking. Despite the anticipated rejection, I was pleasantly surprised that she accepted and was actually excited about it. Wow!

I again was afforded another opportunity to share in her world and extended a fathering moment that would create lifelong memories. I got all dressed up and coordinated my colors with hers and polished up the chariot. We took pictures and went out to eat and attended the prom. Not only did she get a kick out of it, but so did her friends. We danced and we laughed and we had a great time. I did not shadow her and make her experience uncomfortable. I let her go and have fun with her classmates, while I sat at the table and was crowned the old cool dude. When she wanted to dance with me, we did so and when she wanted to dance with others, I rested my feet and caught my breath. What was a defining moment for me is when her friends who didn't have a date, asked me to dance and when her friends chose to accompany she and I at our table. For them to want to chat it up and laugh with me, was flattering and let me know that my attempts at fathering were noticed, appreciated and effective.

These moments must be seized, when they manifest and must not be taken lightly. Too often folk miss out on the numerous opportunities to experience and enjoy one another. I refused to let that narrative play out in my context. They needed it and I longed for it. I had to find ways to let them know how much they meant to me and I had to write a new script for my family tree. The old cycle would be perpetuated, if I did not discover and develop the special moments. I didn't have a playbook to go by, so I created my own. As I considered many families that created scrapbooks and picture albums, it became obvious that they existed because someone chose to create and capture those moments. The still frame was a snippet in time and an occasion where those in the still frames shared a moment. The fathering experiences were our still framed moments and we were able to interact in ways that helped our relationship and that changed the trajectory of and for our family.

We often reflect on such occasions and get great joy in reliving them, through the memories. We now have something to talk about and have something to remember and share with others. This for me was priceless and extremely important. I only hope that they too will continue such, when interacting with their children and that their children's children would do the same. If so, my goal would be reached. To redefine what family is all about and looked like, in the Sanders' clan.

CHAPTER 9

Y.O.L.O.

The quality of your life is heavily determined and influenced by how you live your life. Be mindful, you only live once, so live responsibly.

• • •

The maternal side of my family was raised and reared in a Judaeo-Christian belief. We regularly attended Sunday worship service, Vacation Bible School, Revivals and other special services hosted by our home church. I was brought up to revere God and show decorum in the house of the Lord. My great grandfather was an associate minister in the church that my family attended and he was careful and intentional in instructing his 14 children, to honor the Lord thy God. So for me, it was rather normal and natural to have a belief system, to trust God and to believe in God. This early introduction to faith would serve as the foundation from which my morals, values and beliefs would be built upon. And therefore, would be the foundation from which I would parent and pass on such teachings to my children.

I made it a point, to pray for my children (before and after birth) and to instruct them in the way in which they should go. From a young age, they were taught about Jesus and the importance of making a personal declaration and proclamation of faith. All of my children were baptized, by choice, at a young age and were active in children's ministry.

This was done, not just because it was done with me and because it was expected, but because I knew the importance of having a firm faith foundation. I had sense enough to know, that not only was their eternal destination at hand, but that the quality of their earthly life was contingent upon them having a good set of principles and a well-calibrated moral compass. The lives of black men seemed to be threatened and the likelihood of fathers being a permanent fixture in black homes seemed to be a decreasing reality. I therefore had to ensure that my children would be eternally secured and that I was assured that I did my best to equip them for the world, the wild and the worse. Just in case my presence was interrupted by death, divorce, dope or detention (which was my reality and the milieu in which I had grown up in); I had to get as much into them, as quickly as possible. Lest I continue in the bastardization of our children.

The Christian lifestyle is one that places a great deal of emphasis on faith. Insomuch, that without it, it is impossible to please God and that as a believer, such walk by faith and not by sight. This being the case, I needed to make certain that my children were informed and prepared for life. And for me, what was most important was for them to have a solid faith foundation. Part of responsible parenting, for me, meant to pass on something that would not perish and that was greater than any material possession that I could ever attain. After all, what profits a man to inherit the world and lose his soul? And with all that one could attain in life, nothing could be taken with them and all that they amassed would be left behind and would one day perish.

One principle and precept that I hung my parenting model on, was the passage "A good man, leaves an inheritance to his children's children." The measure of my goodness or the right to be defined as or referred to as a good man was contingent upon what I left to my children and the condition in which I left them. And that of course meant far more than the trinkets and toys that I accumulated in life. No greater heirloom could be given, than that of a firm faith foundation.

Therefore, this became the first talk that I would have with my children and the first step, to breaking the cycle of silence. Faith! After all, You Only Live Once (Y.O.L.O.).

During my younger years, I was afforded the privilege of serving as a youth pastor. As a youth pastor and a young father raising youth, I did my best to stay hip, relevant and abreast of the youth and hip-hop culture. I must admit, this was rather difficult, as youth colloquiums frequently changed and my aging brain couldn't keep up. In addition to the fact that youth made it a point to keep old heads like myself, from peeping their game and by shaming us...telling us how lame we were. Nonetheless, I was able to decipher most of what they embraced, though it was rather difficult to understand their rationale behind things. But that is another story and another book.

One of the phrases that I picked up on, was YOLO. Of course on the surface, one would write this off as just gibberish and conclude this to be another expression of youthful meaningless. But it did have a meaning and the meaning was rather meaningful. As a matter of fact, it was an acronym that stood for, You Only Live Once. After discovering what the acronym stood for, I thought to myself, maybe these youth are listening and they are beginning to understand that life is precious and to be cherished. Maybe they finally understood that their choices mattered and that they have to be more careful, cautious and considerate in life and with their lives. Wishful thinking! Right?

Their usage of the word was just opposite of that. It was their way of saying, life is short and once it's over it's over, so do whatever you want to do and do what you are going to do, quickly. It was almost a mantra, creed and license to live recklessly, carelessly and lawlessly. And guess what, that's exactly what they were committed to doing. The Isley Brothers, "It's yo thang, do what you want to do" had become their theme song and "Turn up" had become their battle cry.

This made my job as youth pastor and daddy, all that more important. I had to help OUR children to see their folly and to try to open their eyes to their faulty thinking. Because in reality, they did have part of it right. You Only Live Once. And at the rate that they were going, that life was going to be short-lived and meaningless. Most importantly, I needed them to understand that though "this life" only offers a one-time around pass, there was another life that had been prepared for them. A life after and beyond this life. I had to warn them, "life is but a vapor, that appears for a moment and then vanishes away." I needed them to understand that "we are destined to die once and then the judgment." On this side of eternity, you only live once. So live it right and live it wisely. And if you live it right and wisely, incorporating and including Christ, you can and will live again. I had to give them something that would steer and save their lives. That something, was a gift. That gift was Jesus.

Daddy Talks...

The greatest gift that I have been given, outside of eternal life, is the gift to give physical life.. The joy of being a parent and in particular, your father, is one that is unparalleled to no other. It warmed my heart, to know that I was chosen to help make and mold life and it is with great honor that I wear the crown and bear the title of daddy. No greater title do I bestow and no other title brings a bigger smile to my face, than that of Dad! This being the case, I must do my very best to ensure that you have the very best. It is my duty and responsibility to make certain that you are well taken of, in this life and the one to come. As I do everything humanly possible to provide for your physical needs, I too must do my part to ensure that your spiritual needs are addressed as well. The greatest gift that I can give to you, is the gift that was given to me…eternal life.

As a human being, we sometimes make mistakes. Our choices are not always good choices and with choices, there are consequences. Those consequences can be rather costly and even deadly. We reap what we sow. In other words, there is fruit inside of every seed and once you plant that seed, the fruit inside will eventually come out. Mankind planted some deadly seeds and as a result, the fruit is deadly. This fruit not only cost us our lives, but cost us relationship with the one who made us and gave us our lives...God. And because God is our creator and in turn our divine parent/father, He cares for us and does not want us to perish. So just as a lovingly parent/father, He makes certain that His children are well taken care and often times finds Himself cleaning up the mess that His children have made. This is what God our Heavenly Father did for us. He saw that we had made a mess out of our lives, by making some bad choices. He noticed that our choices resulted in an eternal death that not only took away the life that He had given, but would separate He and His offspring for eternity. No good parent/father would stand by and just let this happen, without doing something to make it right. God being the good parent/father did just that. He made a decision to rescue his children and instead of placing the penalty and cost on them, which was mandated, He took it upon Himself. He became a sacrifice, so that we would not be sacrificed. And He extends to us an opportunity for our relationship to be restored. This is available through the free gift of eternal life. He did this for us, but we have to choose to accept it. If we choose to accept it, then we are afforded the great benefits of the eternal blessings that have been secured and prepared. However, if we choose to not accept, then the initial penalty of eternal death and separation awaits us. It's our choice. He loves us enough to offer it, we must demonstrate that love toward Him, by accepting it and by accepting Him. This in a nutshell, my children, is what we call the gospel...the good news.

I bring you this good news, because I love you and I don't want to see you perish. I would not be a good father, if I failed to share this with you and allowed you to live your life without being extended the opportunity to meet the one that made it possible for me to make it possible for you. Your earthly and physical life was given to you from your earthly father. Your eternal life is given to you from your heavenly father. And I, your earthly father, introduce you to your heavenly father. This is the greatest gift that I can give and the most important and responsible things that I can do for you. I hope you accept.

I am happy to announce, that my children have gladly received this gift and have stayed and not strayed, away from the family faith. While it is their choice what they would eventually believe, it was my responsibility to coach them along the way. At the time of this writing, they are still actively engaged and involved in the teachings of Christ and are willingly involved in the life of the church and my personal ministry. I am pleased and proud, as it assures and comforts me that they are rooted and grounded in good and Godly principles that will help to guard and govern their lives. I am hopeful that they would remain on this track and devote their lives to these teachings and would in turn pass them on to their offspring. In a time where there are a plethora of philosophies and ideologies, it is rather difficult to keep their attention, while contending with humanistic beliefs and anti-Christ teachings. Though they are very opinionated, like their father, they have chosen to commit themselves to being taught, listening and learning from the teachings that I have committed my life to and find joy in sound and practical instruction. Not only does this warm my heart, I take personal pride and feel a sense of accomplishment in this area. This comforts me, knowing that I have been successful in shaping and molding their spiritual lives and that I have been able to teach them something that my father didn't teach me. For me, this is and was the first step of successful parenting, as I took the role of pouring into them and it has been retained. If I failed in any other area of my parenting, I could rejoice in the fact that I was able to engage in positive parenting, by both breaking the silence and in sharing about the greatest story ever told in the process. With this, I was at least able to be assured that they had something that would ensure their eternal destiny. In addition, they would be equipped with the necessary tools to begin on a path that would usher them onto the path to fulfillment and in a purpose-filled life.

Though I am convinced, beyond a shadow of a doubt, that the Judeo-Christian teachings are absolute and most essential, I am not naïve in knowing that there are others that are equally and passionate in holding to their belief system. To know that my children have maintained these fundamental teachings, I am satisfied in the biblical precepts that affirms, "if you train up a child in the way that they should go, they will not depart." I have taken the necessary steps to train them, at an early age, and pleased that they have not strayed.

For those that choose to read these talks and my thoughts on effective paternal parenting, my hope is that they would use this template to begin healthy dialogue to have healthy and pertinent discussion with their children. Whatever ones faith belief is, this is a great start to having "daddy talks" and breaking the silence. This exchange is not designed to impose my beliefs on the readers, merely to share what I did to break the cycle of silence and to interact with my children. Faith being essential and key to everything that I do, this initial talk is the most natural and logical place to begin. Everything from this point will be built on and centered around these truths and will guide, guard and govern all aspects of their lives. It was my duty to start here and to begin, sooner, rather than later. After all, you only live once. Y.OL.O.

CHAPTER 10

Final Thoughts

I t is my hope that something has been shared within these few pages that has either provided a sense of healing or helped in providing a launching pad to begin your own *Daddy Talks*. I have enjoyed reflecting upon my own journey and am excited that through this writing, others will be afforded a template to use that will maximize their daddy encounters. This reading is far more than what I had, as a new father and has helped me to create a perspective that has been tempered and thought through. Though it was not designed to be a manual, it very well can serve as one. Fathers can use this simple format to engage with their children in ways that will not only impart words of wisdom, but they can create a verbal exchange that can strengthen their relationship. Whatever impact these talks have made upon you and however you choose to use them, the ultimate desire is that they would be the launching pad to restoring and reinforcing relationships. It is such a beautiful site, to see fathers interacting with their children and witnessing the authentic joy that comes from a child having their father actively involved. My earnest desire is that this book will contribute to an explosion of more *Daddy Talks* and daddy time. Happy Fathering!

Bonus material is made available through Daddy Talks website. Should you wish to contact me for coaching, consulting, to book for a speaking engagement or training, feel free e-mail at the address below or visit the website to learn more about services and resources. Also, you can join in a fatherhood movement and engage in a community of other fathers by visiting the *Daddy Talks* site.

www.TheAbundantLifeConsulting.com

TheRev@TheAbundantLifeConsulting.com

www.DaddyTalks.org

Legacy: The Fatherhood Initiative

Through this initiative, fathers are equipped with knowledge and resources that encourages and empowers them to be most effective in their parenting experience. Fathers are coached in the areas of:

➤ Equal Parental Rights

➤ Establishing Joint or Sole Custody

➤ Equitable "Child Support"

➤ Effective Co-parenting

In addition, fathers become a part of a community and a movement, that strongly advocates fatherhood and assist fathers in being present and actively involved in the lives of their children. Through Legacy, training, workshops and seminars offer fathers specific and tangible tools to maximize the paternal parental experience. Tailored and specialized training is also offered to fathers who are detained or immersed in the criminal justice system. Fathers are taught that it is both their right and responsibility to father and neither should be taken lightly. You can find out more information or join the movement by visiting the Facebook page, **Legacy: The Fatherhood Initiative** or at www.DaddyTalks.org

Abundant Life Coaching and Consulting

Many people find themselves stunted from growing in their personal and professional lives, because they have not learned to manage themselves well. When your life is out of control and out of place, the chaos creates catastrophes and cataclysmic consequences. As a result, marriages are dissolved, careers are ended or never started, relationships suffer, depression hinders happiness and people sometimes suffer silently and succumb to their situation. Through *Abundant Life Coaching and Consulting*, services are offered to help people reach their goals, reclaim their lives and reap the benefits of balanced and intentional living. Through guided coaching and goal centered consulting, clients are taught to not merely wait on a breakthrough, rather to create options and opportunities and maximize life.

51540992R00061

Made in the USA
San Bernardino, CA
25 July 2017